OPA'S STORY

H. Bruns

BIOGRAPHY
BY
HUBERT BRUNS

Wer immer strebend sich bemuht den konnen wir erlosen – Goethe
He who always tries his best can be redeemed

© Copyright 2004 Hubert Bruns.

All rights reserved.

No part of this publication may be reproduced, stored in a retrieval system, or transmitted, in any form or by any means, electronic, mechanical, photocopying, recording, or otherwise, without the written prior permission of the author.

Printed in Victoria, Canada

A German version is also available.

Note for Librarians: a cataloguing record for this book that includes Dewey Classification and US Library of Congress numbers is available from the National Library of Canada. The complete cataloguing record can be obtained from the National Library's online database at: www.nlc-bnc.ca/amicus/index-e.html
ISBN 1-4120-3304-7

Bruns, Hubert: October 13, 1923-

TRAFFORD

This book was published on-demand in cooperation with Trafford Publishing.
On-demand publishing is a unique process and service of making a book available for retail sale to the public taking advantage of on-demand manufacturing and Internet marketing. On-demand publishing includes promotions, retail sales, manufacturing, order fulfilment, accounting and collecting royalties on behalf of the author.

Suite 6E, 2333 Government St., Victoria, B.C. V8T 4P4, CANADA
Phone   250-383-6864   Toll-free 1-888-232-4444 (Canada & US)
Fax   250-383-6804   E-mail   sales@trafford.com
Web site www.trafford.com   TRAFFORD PUBLISHING IS A DIVISION OF TRAFFORD HOLDINGS LTD.
Trafford Catalogue #04-1131   www.trafford.com/robots/04-1131.html
10 9 8 7 6

ACKNOWLEDGEMENTS

Sherie Robb – computer typing and layout

Judy Schellenberg – cover design and photography layout

Janet Sankey – editing and proofreading

A troika of labour, ability and love came together. Their dedication made it all possible. Thank you.

Photos: Cover – Janet Sankey
             Title Page – George Blumel
             Last Page – Walter Bruns

COVER

Above – Growing up in the mountains – Arosa, Switzerland

Below – Living now by the ocean – Maple Bay, Vancouver Island, Canada

Dear Reader:

Some time ago my grandchildren arrived. As they grow older they are bound to forget what I was like. So I have written down what I remembered and call it Opa's Story.

It comes to life in Switzerland and stays alive in Germany and Russia during World War II. There were nearly thirty years of overcoming incredible odds and surviving the turmoil of war and its aftermath. Fifty years follow, studying, working and living in the United States and then in Canada.

Adversity dealt kindly with me throughout these years, especially when coping with a stroke in 1988. Ten years later I was able to write again albeit slowly.

The heavens above once determined my orbit; may they set a lucky orbit again for all my loved ones.

Opa

December 2004
Maple Bay

CONTENTS

1. Early Impressions — 1
2. Hitler and the Teenager — 7
3. Munich Before the War — 13
4. World War II — 16
5. Munich under Siege — 21
6. Surrender and Occupation — 30
7. Working for the U.S. Army — 41
8. Studying in Germany and the U.S.A. — 53
9. Immigration to Canada — 65
10. Ups and Downs — 75
11. My Son Walter — 81
12. New Beginnings — 92
13. A Cerebral Incident — 97
14. Adventures — 102
15. The Last Chapter — 119

1

EARLY IMPRESSIONS

I cannot remember much of what was going on around me in the first six years of my life. I have the impression of seeing large houses and hotels with wide wooden balconies, lined up from the village of Arosa in Switzerland to the wide snow fields and the high pass to Davos. I can see the tree line going up to the high mountains. In the summer, I see alpine meadows and look at the cows sounding their bells. Then and later, images are created and I can actually hear the melodious sounds again. In winter and summer, lots of deep blue skies stretch over the big mountains and the landscape, truly a beautiful sight to behold.

Of course it rained but I do not remember that. I was busy playing with my cousins, roaming all over the grounds, which included the large hotel, a number of outbuildings, stables and laundry. Lights, sounds and activities were part of my early days but only some of this remains distinct in memory.

My parents, Heinrich and Lilly Bruns with my two-year old sister Marie-Luise and me had moved to Arosa in 1924 from Nordenburg, East Prussia. We lived in my grandmother's house and my mother worked in the office of the large Kurhotel Arosa which was owned by my grandmother, Omi Jacobi. This hotel had become a sanitarium for tuberculosis patients. It is interesting to note that my grandmother knew the author, Thomas Mann who lived in Arosa while doing research for his book, *The Magic Mountain*.

My grandmother was quite a matriarch, very pleasant but not to be trifled with. I was repeatedly told not to run my wound-up toy in any of the hallways but I could not resist. One day she caught me and because I used a bad word, dragged me to a sink, pressed me firmly against it and proceeded to wash my face and mouth with laundry soap. My memory of her begins to recede, but the taste and smell of laundry soap in my mouth still comes back vividly whenever I am near this soap.

I am reasonably sure that I was not an out and out brat at the time, but did try to get into and participate in all the interesting work as done by the help on the estate, such as snow removal on the flat hotel roof. Once, on the roof alone, I picked up one of the wide square shovels used to cut large snow blocks. Using the shovel, you could easily slide the block of snow to and over the edge. You must promptly twist the handle to flip the load. I had noticed the motion but paid insufficient attention and nearly missed twisting the loaded shovel, almost catapulting myself off the roof. For the first time, I experienced a sharp fear gripping my heart. In years to come I have again experienced some strong and immediate fear, so I remember.

School does not seem to have done much for me. I can only recall a few words of a song and apple cider being made in the school yard. No writing or spelling seems to have taken place but more winter skiing was organized. My father was seldom in Arosa and my mother was working. In the evening, I would be at home with my mother and try to do at least some homework. No wonder that in Grade Four of Marburg Public School, my uncle and the teacher were amazed that I could hardly read or write. Only after tutoring was I allowed to get into the academic stream and start the first grade of high school.

In the last winter before leaving Arosa, several resort activities took place on the frozen "Obersee", among them the annual race of skijoring (a horse with or without a rider pulling a skier). My mother won this race twice. She also broke her leg twice doing this dangerous sport! As well, she used to ski with friends over the high pass from Arosa to Davos. What with one aunt being a high-diving champion and my mother so athletic, it appears that I may have gotten some of the right genes.

The small-gauge railroad from Chur to Arosa followed a rather steep, narrow twisting road. From Arosa down to the first railway stop at Rutli, the resort would close the road due to heavy snow and very little traffic. They would hard-pack the surface, then bank and ice all the turns, creating a good bobsled run. A friend of mine and I observed the grown-ups getting ready to start a bobsled race, adjusting seating and steering arrangements and generally milling about. Both of us had noticed a two-seater made with rope handles which looked just right, so we took a running start, jumped in and took off with my friend on the rear brakes and me steering with the two rope handles. We started going awfully fast but the trick was to go fast enough into and around the banked turns, not to slide down and into them, but not to shoot off a turn either. Hollering and shouting gleefully with excitement, we made it to

Rutli but then simmered down when we were given a severe scolding by both our mothers as they took us back to Arosa.

I think I was lucky in early life and as well throughout all these years. One should not tempt fate and the gods by claiming that the lucky ones are consistently fortunate in life. My mother simply could not realize her potential in her life. She went through two world wars, two complete inflations, a wide-spread depression and long-lasting poverty. The man she wanted to choose was killed; the man she married was not of her substance. She had, altogether, a difficult life but one filled with kindness, humour and a stiff upper lip.

In 1932, paradise was lost. Grandmother's Kurhotel Arosa went bankrupt and she lost houses and other real estate as the Depression began to settle in. All family members had to leave for Germany. My father had already left. My mother, sister and I stayed for a few months only with a girlfriend in Northern Germany. In early 1933, Mother managed to board my sister with the Enders family in Ulm and me with an uncle in Marburg. She herself was able to get a housekeeping job with another uncle's widow in Cannes, France.

I was 9 years old when I arrived in Marburg and stayed two years until 1935. I can only vaguely remember a tearful good-bye at the train station. Other than that I adjusted well and responded to my uncle, Kreispfarer Schmidmann, who was in charge of a diocese and the Lutheran Church near Marburg Castle.

The reason why I remember him and this time so vividly is that to me he embodied being a Christian. By that I mean that he was one without the touch of religious certainty. In word or gesture he never became sanctimonious and was always down to earth. I have found that there are not many truly genuine people, especially in the clergy but he was one. It was the measure of the man to dispense with overt religious instruction. He and his wife treated me with kindness, affection and humour, no doubt with a bit of difficulty at times. Because I lived in the manse, I was expected to appear at church at least on Sundays and I did so most of the time. I was never sharply remonstrated with and only once did Aunt Elisabeth slap me across the face. I do not remember why but I do recall the sharp sting caused by her rather large wedding ring on my cheek. I did not realize it at the time but the two years I spent in Marburg have given me a lifetime of nice memories.

In 1933, the 10 - 14 year old youngsters and the 14 - 18 year old teenagers were asked by parents to join the Hitler Youth. I wanted to be with my neighbourhood friends and to join their activities. My uncle did not see any reason why not. Years later, he may have changed his mind as the times changed. At any rate, I happily went along with whatever took place because it was something new and exciting. There was the time a unit moved in firm unison, marching and singing, towards the Civic Square. There was the sound of rhythmic singing, the unison of feet on the pavement, all in one disciplined forward and contagious motion. If one has never marched in a disciplined column but at least listened, one understands the fascination for the force of solidarity and for the noticeable stirring of emotions.

In the Fall of 1933, the Depression was in full force and a number of agencies collected money, goods and services. My Hitler Youth unit was given tin cups to collect coins for the needy on street corners. We marched to the army parade grounds and lined up to be handed cups one at a time by the teenager in command. When he stepped in front of me to hand over a cup, something in me happened and I just said, "No!" He was startled and responded, "You are doing what?" But again I said, "No", whereupon he told me to step in front of the line and obey. When I refused, he yanked off my kerchief and dismissed me in front of the entire unit. Perhaps then and now I just do not easily accept commands unless explained properly to my understanding.

I ran through the streets all the way home, completely beside myself in rage, crying and sobbing without let-up. When I got to my uncle, he could not help smiling a bit and explained that really a good deed was intended. I could not see it that way then but later had a feeling that my sense of dignity had been violated. The same feeling but for a very different reason, a sense of outrage, went through me when fighting once with one boy on the pavement while some other bigger ones stood about peeing on us.

My two years in Marburg ended in the summer of 1935. My uncle was not a substitute father for me but certainly came close to being one in precept and example. School began to interest me but writing to my mother was difficult. Being occasionally allowed in my uncle's study, I found interesting books and began to do some reading. Church bells and the singing of the congregation are still with me as are some of the words of the hymns. Altogether, a very good fortune allowed me to have been in Marburg.

2

HITLER AND THE TEENAGER

My mother got a part-time clerical job and worked to upgrade herself to typist and stenographer. My father had obtained a minor civil service position. He increasingly suffered from epileptic seizures. He also had a drinking problem and eventually had to be hospitalized. I saw very little of him and nothing later on. My parents were divorced in 1938.

At last, in the summer of 1935, Mother, Madi (Marie-Luise) and I were together again in a very nice suburb of Munich, one hour from downtown by streetcar. Very soon, being the only wage earner, my mother could not maintain such a place and we had to move to a small three bedroom flat next to the main railway station. There were always two students in the bedrooms, Mother and Madi in the third and I on the sofa in the living room next to the stove. There was one toilet, a sink with cold water only and a small kitchen without a refrigerator.

My mother lost the privilege of money and social status. "One never talks about money whether you have it or not", she used to say. She judged herself and others by what was bred into her and she remained true to herself throughout the trials and disasters she had to endure. I tried to emulate her and cheer her up.

My school hours were from 8:00 to 1:00 and she worked until 6:00. There was no lunch break or cafeteria for a traditional, substantial noontime meal. She managed to locate a daycare centre next to my school run by Catholic sisters. They taught her to sew and she actually produced my first jacket and pants. More importantly, the sisters allowed me to have lunch every day. There I was, in second year of high school (Grade 7), eating with pre-schoolers. I found it difficult to accept. As in Marburg, some loss of dignity was felt.

I remember the two of us at home in good company and conversation, with her the way she was and I learning by osmosis, while she was mending or sewing. She was great fun to be with, having a very good sense of humour. She tried to diminish the heroic happenings of the time, saying that she would prefer less heroics and more normal times.

Although getting a bicycle and riding home every day, I still spent afternoons reading in a library, sometimes ending up with several books. I used to read quickly and could retain well. After eating supper, I would recount the contents to my mother while she did mending and housework. She would point out and explain things, especially history. I liked these discussions very much but managed to avoid the matter of homework.

I liked school and did reasonably well at most subjects, with my favourite subjects being physical education, history and geography. Most others required effort which I did not make often enough. Only later on did I realize that to do better in life means to do more. My sister, Madi, had to consistently make more of an effort in life in order to enjoy the good parts.

The Munich Kunstler Haus was built in the 1900s for and by a group of prominent artists including painters, sculptors, writers and composers as a gathering place for entertainment, food, music, lectures, etc. It was located in the heart of Munich and consisted of a four-sided, two-storey high building enclosing a large rectangular tiled courtyard with a large heavy wooden door leading to a small side street. It was usually kept closed and a small side door was used to walk in and out to the sidewalk of the short side street.

In 1938, renovations were made under the auspices of the Reich's Chancellor and President, Adolf Hitler, then increasingly referred to as the Fuerer. A construction company set up an office in the Kunstler Haus with my mother working there as a secretary. During the summer school holidays of 1938, I hung about because there was lots to observe.

One day, a phone call came into the office advising that Hitler wished to inspect the progress made and to tell the work crew to stay out of the building until further notice. They left and the architect and others, as well as some plain-clothes men, assembled and so did I, moving to the small door and keeping it open, standing to one side. I had about fifteen minutes before Hitler was to arrive. I was not aware of it but later realized that security was not enforced then that much.

Then two beautiful, black convertible Mercedes drove up and stopped in front of the courtyard door with the driver and Hitler in front. A non-commissioned SS officer jumped out of the second car and ran to open the door of the first car. Hitler stepped out, turned to the small door and went into the courtyard, all in one quick, decisive motion and then greeted some dignitaries.

I stayed in the background only twenty feet from Hitler, watching his easy conversation with the architect and others. I could not make out the words but watched his smile. The obvious detectives stayed together but the SS men actually played featherball in his presence, tossing the ball back and forth. I was very surprised, but on other occasions I think I found an explanation. Hitler must have been able to hypnotize himself as well as others. I felt he was totally within himself all the time, projecting whatever he wanted to accomplish for himself or others. Anything else stayed in the background or did not exist. After talking, he turned very abruptly and started the inspection with the entourage, some detectives and me in the rear. The SS men stayed behind and kept playing featherball.

I had explored the Kunstler Haus very well but evidently Hitler knew the layout too. We arrived at an open space in front of one building with a fenced-in enclosure, allowing a view of the facade without being seen from the outside. Hitler looked at it without turning to a high-ranking official in uniform who stood at attention on his left. From about twenty feet I could not make out what was said but I picked up the very sharp and harsh tone of voice. I will never forget, remembering the official standing there literally shaking in his riding boots, a grown man being truly afraid.

Hitler was always in the lead, all others following behind. I wanted to shake his hand but would have to wait for an opportunity. It came when the procession moved through a quite narrow hallway intersected at right angles by others. I went through one and stood there waiting. When he came forward, I stuck my hand out and he shook it with a weak handshake, almost not seeing me. It seemed as though he was not really there. I had confronted him very suddenly but no sign of surprise showed. The procession then moved on but one detective touched me on my shoulder and said, "Get lost!" I stayed away from any more of the inspection for awhile.

One of the buildings contained large rooms and high ceilings with walls which were in the process of receiving large murals. A scaffold made of wide boards was up close to the ceiling and a ladder was left leaning against it. As before, I moved through parallel halls to dodge detectives and to stay closer to Hitler. I misjudged and had to disappear quickly. I turned into the mural room, climbed the ladder and lay flat on my stomach on the boards. When they came in I was looking down through the cracks between the boards, directly at Hitler.

Even as I write, the details come back in full memory. My heart was pounding and I was truly scared. I knew that if anyone looked up and perceived a difference in the cracks against the white ceiling, the detectives would aim and shoot at me without hesitation. I did not think then as I do now, but something told me I was in true mortal danger. They left the room and I knew I had been very lucky. I left the room too but only after awhile.

For some time I kept my distance. I could clearly see Hitler's face and hear his voice. I was fascinated by what went on so close to Germany's idol but I still wanted to be closer. Then an opportunity presented itself. Without really thinking, I moved close to the small door and waited. As usual, Hitler would say a few words in the courtyard after an inspection. He then turned as if in the middle of a sentence and started to walk quickly and decisively towards the door where I waited.

In the meantime, the two Mercedes outside on the short side street had attracted a sizeable crowd, who were quite sure that Hitler was in the Kunstler Haus. A few policemen kept the crowd lined up on the other side of the street.

Hitler kept on coming as I opened the door. He stepped through and stood facing the crowd. I stepped through as well, now standing by his side. The crowd roared and broke into applause. He smiled, repeatedly raised his arm and acknowledged the people. As he did so, I kept looking at the multitude, seeing and hearing them, transfixed by emotions. For a fleeting moment, I thought of also raising my arm but thought better of it.

I had blocked the SS men beside me but they would not make a move, very likely because Hitler and I were now in full view of the assembled crowd. For several minutes both of us stood there until he took the few steps across the sidewalk to his car. However, I moved faster, enough to get my hand on the car door. I opened it, let him sit down, closed it and said something to the effect of please return. Again, as before, he was not really aware of me and said nothing to me. I looked at him as the SS men got into their car and then both moved off. I never met Hitler again.

I turned into the Kunstler Haus, my heart full of what I had witnessed in the last few weeks, especially the moments standing at Hitler's side in adulation. There must have been any number of photos taken then and I would love to have one. Many violent things began to happen over the next several years but they did not completely overshadow the images of these weeks. They are part of my history. Hopefully, competent historians will judge events more evenly in the future.

3

MUNICH BEFORE THE WAR

The main Munich railway station was situated a block away from our flat. Depending on the wind, the sounds and smells could be noticed easily, especially at night. I often spent time there and over the years picked up a real liking for everything connected with railroads. I would fall asleep with the sound of a whistle in my ears, dreaming of far away places.

To make some spending money, I went onto platforms where long distance trains arrived and approached people having sizeable luggage to carry. I had to be circumspect to avoid trouble with the official porters so I greeted my people cheerfully. One day, I found a key with a squared hole used to open outside rail cars and compartments, as well as for registering individual seats.

In the summer of 1939, I completed the fifth year of high school (Grade 9) and decided that that amount of schooling would do. I had not failed any subjects but would have had to do much better in senior grades and endure four more years of school to pass the final matriculation. Instead, I entered a three-year commercial apprentice program with the BMW Company to become a journeyman. I convinced my mother that I should start working and making money if only for 40 reichsmarks a month to start.

Before doing that, however, I got it into my head to apply for a passport to travel and visit my English relatives who were farming in Kenya. How to get there or how to pay for it was not quite clear to me. I think I had the idea that the relatives would pay but I never got a reply. My mother kept humouring me but I finally gave up. At least I got my passport without having a parent sign for it, something that at the time took some doing. I still have it, complete with a swastika emblem.

Instead of going to Kenya, I wanted to visit my grandmother in Wiesbaden before going to work at BMW. There just was not enough money for this but I discovered how to go anyway, by hitchhiking. Long distance truckers maintained an office where a trucker could find a list of loads going to different cities. Inter-city trucking took two drivers who could select the city they wanted. Hanging around this office, all I had to do was talk to the driver going my way. Hitchhiking was of course forbidden but most of the drivers I approached let me come aboard. If not, I had to go home and start again the next day. How I managed to convince my mother that this was safe I cannot remember, but I did arrive safe and sound in Wiesbaden.

In the summer of 1939, most long distance trucking was conscripted to haul material to the "West Wall", designed to strengthen the German-French frontier. Suddenly, I found myself unable to hitchhike back to Munich. It seemed to me that I had to go by train but how was I to pay for it? I was determined not to ask some distant relatives or bother my elderly grandmother. I was bound and determined to see the problem through without help and without a train ticket. I knew that just walking the coaches and dodging into toilets would not keep the conductors from noticing me, especially since the coaches were checked after every stop. Every conductor had this special key for the outside of a compartment, setting keys for any seat occupied, and locking it after checking tickets. I had found the key to get home.

I bought a ten-cent ticket which was used to get onto platforms. I boarded the Frankfurt Express and kept behind the conductor as he started to make his first round. When I got to a compartment with an empty seat, I looked at the register of seats, picked one, inserted my key for it, opened the compartment door and sat down, hoping that nobody had observed closely.

I tried to be as nonchalant as possible but I could not prevent my excitement. Then the fateful moment came and the conductor entered having first glanced at the register. "Anyone boarded?" he asked. Nobody said anything. He backed out, closing the door behind him but not without looking slightly my way.

Three more stops at Stuttgart, Ulm and Augsburg had to be endured and they did not get much better except that I thought the conductor had gotten used to me. I was again very lucky and relieved when I finally vaulted over the barrier at the Munich Station, waving and acting as if I had to follow someone, leaving quickly. I promised my mother that I would not ride a train again without a paid ticket.

4

WORLD WAR II

World War II started on September 1, 1939 with Germany claiming that shooting had taken place and that Poland would have to be answered. On the radio that day I heard Hitler's announcement: "I have therefore decided to shoot back!" The exact same phrase, "I have therefore decided..." was used by J. F. Kennedy in 1962, announcing the imminent attack on Cuba and Russia. In one case, one man had gone down taking millions of dead with him. The other one luckily averted disaster for all of us.

My junior apprenticeship at BMW started in the Fall of 1939 without much learning or excitement save for war happenings, such as the complete division of Poland, the occupation of all of Norway and the fall of Holland, Belgium and France. By the beginning of 1941, it looked like England might surrender because of increasing sea and air attacks. My mother was working. Madi learned to become a seamstress and I was at BMW in various departments including a fully equipped machine shop for one month. I liked to work with my hands and wanted to become a mechanic, but I observed my friends there, some of whom had real aptitude.

The first two years of the war did not directly affect the civilian population much, except for the twenty-four hour shifts in factories such as BMW and some food rationing. We were poor before the war and still were after it started. Because of rationing, we ate mostly fried potatoes and onions. All Germans were under the constant influence of radio, newspapers, newsreels and pronouncements from on high. All of it was orchestrated by an expert, Dr. Joseph Goebels.

When I found out that my three-year apprenticeship could be shortened, I wanted to volunteer. My mother refused to consent at first but then agreed with my arguments. I argued that I would have to wait one or more years, that the war would likely be over before then and that I would lose out on better advancements later on. You cannot guess what will lead to survival under war circumstances. You have to take chances. My mother and I took them and made it all the way to old age! I went into the German Army in April, 1941 at 17 years of age.

It turned out that I ended up in a special quartermaster unit which consisted mostly of trucks. Proper military training was then deferred in order to speed up preparation for the assault on Russia. Supplies, especially gasoline in full barrels, were moved to the east in huge columns that started in Germany and were timed carefully to reach Poland and the Russian border precisely by the end of June, 1941. The German offensive began June 22, 1941. My truck and I crossed the line four days later, closely following the tanks.

Tanks, ammunition and supplies had to be replaced as the "Blitzkrieg" continued to move into Russia during the summer, pushing back and surrounding the Russian armies repeatedly. We then started to pick up supplies at railheads. However, trains moved slowly because all the tracks had to be changed due to the wider rail gauge used in Russia. From there, our trucks moved to the forward lines and into artillery positions.

The Fall season approached and with it the rains. Most of the German front slowed down. We had started in Lithuania and worked our way past Smolensk toward Moscow. Foot-deep mud made roads almost impassable even when smaller trees were cut by hand and laid alternately to make some sort of a roadbed.

When the ground froze, we moved again but slowly. Around the time of my 18th birthday, I entered a three-storey wooden building having outside landings which also served as toilets, each with short lengths of pipe and an open concrete trough extending the length of the building. I had a piece of paper in my hand from a German newspaper to be used as toilet paper, which announced in the headline that the Russian campaign was practically won. I felt that something was truly amiss but I did not dwell on it because a cold blast kept coming up the pipe.

As we continued toward Moscow along the rail line from Vyazma going east, conditions deteriorated badly. It became bitterly cold. We had no antifreeze and had to build fires under oil pans if stopped for any length of time. We had no winter tires, proper winter clothing or winter boots. I was covered all over with lice and scratched myself even at night, and as a result was covered with scabs. It became too much. Halfway between Vyazma and Moscow we had stopped for a few days and I was told that no action would be likely. I found out that I could get into a delousing hut so I asked permission to go there for a proper shower and clean-up.

Before the war, I can say that I was well built and in very good shape. For example, horsing around after our tenants took a break, I picked up a student and tossed him bodily on the bed which then collapsed, to my mother's dismay. Now, however, I was coughing badly, cold inside and out, itching all over, and being truly miserable as never before. But more was in store for me on this lonely, dark and cold evening.

I trudged along for some kilometers to get to the hut but it was too late. The sergeant in charge told me to come back the next morning because the steam had already been turned down. I tried to persuade him to let me stay overnight but he insisted that I had to go back to my unit. I kept pleading and he finally relented, saying that I could go to a nearby first aid station and ask to stay until morning. The sergeant there said I could stay and sleep on the floor together with the lightly wounded. I was exhausted and went out like a light.

At midnight an alarm was sounded and everyone was to immediately get up and climb into trucks. I obeyed, half asleep, and the truck roared off. Russian and Siberian reserves had started to counterattack the previous day. The truck came to a rail siding and all of us got out and into a boxcar, thankfully with a heated stove to thaw us out. At about noon, arriving in Vyazma we got out and were lined up in single file for medics and doctors to check us over. When one got to me he wanted to know what was the matter with me since I had no wounds but then he looked at my teeth, and at the obvious bad state of my general condition. He ordered me to be moved to Smolensk for badly needed dental work. At the clinic in Smolensk, I was told that I had scurvy and the work on my teeth could not be done there yet and I was ordered to go to Krakow in Poland. The train from Smolensk took 76 hours, stopped every so often mostly at night because of partisans shooting it up. Sometimes the steam connections between coaches burst, with the ice on the windows an inch thick.

Other times the coach became so hot that the lightly wounded and I stripped almost completely. It went through my mind that this 76 hour train ride could certainly be endured because it travelled west, towards home.

By the time the train reached Krakow, I had developed a high fever. I was taken off the train and taken by ambulance to the hospital. The doctors discovered that I had active tuberculosis so I was transferred to a sanatorium in Germany for three months. Years later, I met a friend from my former unit. He told me that it had been virtually wiped out at the very same time that I had insisted on staying overnight in order to be deloused the next day.

Once more I was very lucky. At the sanatorium, I mostly slept in an open room under several blankets. At Christmas, and on her birthday, December 26, my mother came to visit and decided to go for a one-day hike, saying it would be good for me, but I was not up to it. Physically, I got better soon except for having lost most of my teeth. Mentally, I started to think again, something I had done very little of, what with the constant pressure of staying alive. I thought somewhat vaguely I should pay more attention to what could be called the seriousness of normal life, and in particular to get more schooling. At least something like this was in the back of my mind, ready to jell. Before being re-assigned, I was given a complete physical. It was determined that because I had had TB and was only 18, I should be deferred for one year. I had been in the army for one year, one month and five days.

5

MUNICH UNDER SEIGE

In the Spring of 1942, I went to visit a distant relative, Goertitz, in Berlin but did not see that much of the city or its surroundings. What I saw in comparison with Munich impressed me very much. It helped that they were having a beautiful early spring. People spent time strolling on weekends through the wide promenades and parks. There was no indication of war except for uniformed soldiers and some civilians and families wearing armbands with the yellow star of David. Not having seen them before I asked about this and was told that the Jews were about to be relocated to the East. I was not given any further explanation but had known of the official government policy. I did not get any more details until much later.

My sister, Madi had joined the German version of the WAC, the Women's Auxiliary Corps, and was stationed at German Army headquarters in East Prussia, close to Hitler's bunker. She had been on leave in Munich and returned by train, via Berlin. I met her there but had only a short visit before her 12-hour trip to East Prussia and took her to the train station.

The outdoor station platforms were open-ended, and although we arrived very early, our platform was already completely crowded by soldiers in uniform having to go back to their units. It was obvious that a chance to have a seat was out of the question. The best she could do was squeeze in and stand.

Some action had to be taken! I had not forgotten my train lore and I had kept my key. I told her to stay as visible as possible and to look for me in one of the coaches as they arrived. As I walked off the platform and down to the rail bed, toward the empty coaches coming in, I counted them to line one up as close as possible to her position. I made my decision and jumped up off the rail bed, caught the high door handle and hung on, got out my four-cornered key, unlocked the door and went in. The coaches slowly came to a stop. I opened a window and waved. Madi was reasonably close to the door I had unlocked and fought her way toward me and into the compartment. She got a seat and so was able to sit in relative comfort throughout the long trip. However, I had trouble getting out through the aisle and down to the door, as soldiers were still storming in. They must have observed my action and were inclined to throw me out. However, I managed to scramble out through a window.

I decided to go home to Munich where I had some friends and my mother had her flat. She was now a secretary, being able by now to read and write shorthand reasonably well. Through her, I got a job in the Bavaria Film Kunst, a movie studio where I was put in charge of summarizing old movies so as to come up with average budgets for standard sequences. Shortly after I started, I found out that I could try and sit for a special senior high school matriculation exam. As part of this program for German veterans, equivalent to the U.S. GI Bill of Rights, I could be, if I passed, accepted by any German university for Business Administration, Economics, Philosophy, Law, etc. but not, for example, Medicine.

There was my chance at a higher education. My boss let me spread my textbooks all over my office and desk and let me study more or less most of the time. I organized the evenings by asking my mother to type and produce excerpts. My cousin Lore, who studied at the University of Munich and stayed with us, made numerous précis from her notes and spent hours cramming with me, as my mother did as well. It was a true team effort and it paid off.

It turned out that my mental capacity was open to enlargement and I could concentrate much better than before. Now by studying I learned how to study, something that should have been done first in the early years by my mother. But my mother could not do it then. At 19 years of age, I was already a veteran with a high school diploma though the latter contained a proviso. Nevertheless, I was happy when I remembered how easily and well students talked to each other. Now I could begin to think and talk like that. I was allowed to enter Munich University for the study of Business Administration and Economics in the Fall of 1943.

In the early part of 1944, it became more difficult to study. Increasing air raids caused cancellation or rescheduling of lectures, sometimes held in suburbs. Essential production was still at a peak due to enormous efforts made by the population, including the "guest arbeiter" ("guest workers") not all of whom were conscripted. Students were allowed to stay for essential courses and had to keep up their grades or be dropped for military or civilian service. Living conditions deteriorated and to continue to study became impossible.

On July 11, 12 and 13, 1944, the heaviest daytime air raids so far caused widespread damage to the core of the city. All water, gas and hydro lines were damaged or had to be disconnected on the first day. On the second day, many buildings continued to burn. It looked like Munich would be completely destroyed.

The flat that mother, Madi and I lived in was on the second floor of a small house. It adjoined a six-storey building made of concrete and the basement was used as an air raid shelter. It had wooden support beams, chairs, benches and two heavy steel doors leading out and up to the street. There was a large courtyard connecting with the basement where tires, inner tubes, solvents, etc. were stored.

This substantial building was located close to the train station and was the Munich home office of the Continental Tire and Rubber Company. For air raids, shelter space was readily available here, including for the tenants in our small house next door. All of us there were happy to be in a well-made shelter. Even if a bomb were to hit, it could not possibly penetrate through five concrete floors and the basement. On July 11 and 12 no bombs had hit these two houses. Down the street a number of fires started in attics but they could easily be put out as all the attics were completely emptied and a thin layer of concrete put in. A small bicycle pump and pails of water produced a primitive but very effective water hose. I helped the nearby neighbours to make use of them.

The next day, the 13th of July, I got up, still tired and grimy. At home we did not have a bathtub, only a sink with emergency water. I cleaned up as well as I could and put on a fresh pair of pants and shirt. Even while doing that I felt somewhat odd under the circumstances. Later on it occurred to me that I must have prepared to lay out my clothes to die.

As I finished dressing, the third air raid started with police cars sounding the alarm and the first anti-aircraft guns started to fire. The first of several hundred bombers approached Munich, with their tail formations still above Stuttgart. As on the two days before, the frightening sound of exploding bombs started to come nearer. A latecomer off the street and I ran two and three steps at a time down the staircase and made it through the double steel doors into our shelter. In there were about fifty people. At one end, thirty of them were standing against the wall separating the shelter from the storage basement. About twenty people, mostly from the neighbourhood, were sitting in their usual places. Only candles gave some light. The second inside steel door was moving soundlessly from the detonations outside. The almost soundproof shelter seemed to sway a bit and hardly anybody said a word.

I had moved to my usual chair close to my mother and sister, but the chair was taken by the fourteen year old boy living with his parents downstairs in our small house. I asked him to move but he started a fuss. I could have forced him but I did not because people there were already upset. Someone moved another empty chair toward my mother and I sat down close to her and my sister. Unlike her, I did not have a flashlight in my hand or a gas mask on my face as required. Instead, I flipped it by the straps and crossed my legs, being reasonably pleased at having made it into the shelter.

At that moment, a heavy bomb exploded. As seen from above, it must have glanced off and dropped past the six-storey high building, hit the yard and then went into the yard basement, exploding there with a delayed fuse. It blew a large opening into the shelter of broken-up pieces of concrete, killing some thirty people who were standing against that wall and injuring some twenty more.

I cannot really remember if I actually heard the explosion. Rather it seemed as if something solid went straight into my brain. Next, I felt I was about to suffocate and called out my sister's name before losing consciousness. Her hands immediately went to where my head was covered by loose debris and aided by her flashlight, uncovered my head. I managed just barely to breath in some air as my mother cleaned up my face, while I desperately tried to move my arms. My face, mouth and eyes were covered with dust and I could see nothing. Madi fled to get help through the interconnected air raid shelters.

Together with my mother, I managed to move my arms a little but realized that I was truly trapped. My hands felt what seemed to be a large, heavy piece of concrete, partly on my lap and partly on my thigh. I felt tremendous pressure on my right thigh but was able to wiggle my right toes. My leg soon went numb and I felt no more pain. I could then make out that the yard basement had ignited and flames began to move into the shelter together with heavy smoke from burning tires.

More rubber material fed the fire and more flames continued to advance into our shelter. Fortunately, the heavy smoke went up through the hole that had blown open. Those who were trapped cried out for help but burned in agony and fell silent. The flames got closer and my face started to get hotter. There was no escape. I knew it and so did my mother. She then said in a calm and steady voice, "I will die with you here". I told her she would have to leave as my sister had. But we were lucky; the flames did not get any closer and only my face got singed a bit. From there on in we talked about things in general, still in a calm and collected manner, there being nothing else to do, for about one hour. The survivors, including my sister, had left and all noise in the shelter abated. Finally, a rescue team came in through the small emergency openings cut between every shelter.

I always appreciated my mother not only for what she did for me but as well for what she was, a person of true substance. She would explain things in line with her standards. If she had to accommodate others, she would revert to her principles. It is owing to her personality that I began to attain some mental and emotional maturity and perhaps achieved a bit of wisdom. As I recall the hour being together in the bombed-out shelter, I again marvel at her strength of character, determination and ability to cope under extreme duress. She never faltered or broke down. All through these years I have tried to follow her example.

The rescue team in the shelter began to move the heavy beam, concrete blocks and other debris out of the way. In trying to help with this, my hands touched the fourteen year old's head, crushed by the weight of the beam and concrete. He died sitting where I would have sat, with his chest on my thigh, saving it from being crushed. The men then took me by the shoulders, dragged me through an emergency opening and out to the street. I stood up very shakily, on one leg with some support. My mother came right behind. She told me afterwards that I looked very bad, covered in blood, as bad as the corpses looked when she later had to identify them, including the young boy.

I was taken by ambulance to a temporary first aid station in a very large four-storey underground shelter which was used to store vats of beer. A doctor examined me and announced that very little injury had been done except for some burns, muscle deformation of my thigh and some cuts. The latter would have to be stitched but without freezing as it should be saved for more important cases. The doctor said it would hurt, especially on my cut lip.

He was right! I was laid out on a heavy table, with one helper holding down my legs and the other two each pinning down my head and shoulders. He proceeded to put the needle through my lip three times and about twelve times through my scalp. The scalp hurt very much, the lip even more. My eyes followed his hands as the curved needle went in and he held his fingers to my lip to pull the thread tight. I still see this in my mind sometimes when I touch my lip or look at the small scar.

I was told that this emergency shelter was filled to capacity and I should move in a few days. My mother found out where I was and came to see how I was doing. She looked absolutely dreadful and white as a sheet when she asked how I was. I wanted to get her to smile but she did so only after I moved aside the blanket saying that my right leg was just fine and uncovered it. Only then was she able to relax a little bit.

After my mother had left me by the ambulance, she had to go through several horrible ordeals. One of the rescue men who helped me to get out of the shelter required her to go to the building passage where they had lined up the corpses from the shelter we had been in. She had to identify some, including the boy that sat in my chair. She then helped to throw mattresses down into the street from our flat, then on top of them everything else that had not yet burned and been destroyed.

After a few days in the emergency shelter, I got a ride to a friend's place. I finally had a chance to have a bath and wash my clothes. They were soaked with the boy's blood and only very little of mine. On July 16, I took a train to Ulm to stay with my mother's sister and her husband who was a doctor. He confirmed that only minor things happened. A small artery in my lungs burst and caused a bit of blood to be coughed up but that stopped after a few weeks.

I came back to Munich where my mother and sister were now assigned a small flat which they furnished with the remnants of our belongings. We were together again. Air alarms and attacks became more frequent yet still the population was determined to persevere under increasing hardships. Studying became irrelevant; the search for food and other essentials, such as heating oil, was more important. Christmas and New Year's Eve 1944 increased the heavy shadows cast on the future.

6

SURRENDER AND OCCUPATION

The last major battle of the war took place close to Germany's western border in Belgium. In that encounter, the Americans had to retreat with heavy casualties but the Germans could not keep advancing past some breakthroughs. One of the German units taking part there was an SS Panzer unit. One year later some of them were hanged as explained in later chapters. The collapse at the Battle of the Bulge made it certain that resistance could not be continued for long. The government promise of vastly superior and devastating weapons was increasingly not believed anymore. All civilian males were armed and organized into a "Folks Sturm" to fight alongside regular German army units inside Germany. It was time for me to leave Munich and try to obtain some food. I moved to a farm south-east of Munich, near Bad Aibling. It consisted of several fields, pigs, cows and horses. A silo, granary and general warehouse completed a large flour mixer and a sizeable bakery. The farmer next door ran a creamery. Every week I put together as many supplies as I could and brought them to Munich with a small borrowed motorbike.

Unlike the savage fighting close to and around Berlin, German units in the West fell back under the steady advance of the allied forces, and cities such as Stuttgart and Ulm were occupied with little difficulty. In Munich, food supplies became scarce and unreliable and increasingly non-existent. Forcibly confined inmates in large institutions and camps began to starve as food supplies simply ran out. After months or years of rationing, inmates now started to die from complications caused by malnutrition, among them my own father, who died near Munich in the last weeks of the war.

Law and order began to disintegrate after five years of enormous efforts and sacrifice. It became increasingly difficult to get my food parcels into Munich to my mother and sister. Although there were more than 10 million conscripted foreign labourers in Germany, on the whole they did not start to get out of hand. Discipline had been maintained except at the very end. Severe penalties were imposed and enforced especially during the blackouts.

Throughout the last few weeks of the war and into October, 1945, I continued to stay with the farmer. He really was a shrewd businessman, running his sizeable enterprise with top efficiency. He got up at 4:00, got the three bakers going, got me up at 5:00 and into the pigsty cleaning out 42 pigs which took more than one hour, while he took a short rest. In spite of all the food at the farm, breakfast was accompanied simply with ersatz coffee, not the real thing. I then worked in the warehouse until lunch and into supper, and afterwards, more often than not, helped to load the truck until evening, six days a week. I was out like a light by 9:00 every night.

I have never again done such hard physical work. Together with a second man, we each had to lift a sack of flour which was 200 pounds, German pounds that is, take it off a ramp and carry it into the bakery. I learned to work hard under all kinds of conditions, to stay with it and not to make excuses to myself or others. This was difficult to do at times. Next to the farm buildings, animal and human sewage drained into a concrete septic container measuring 25 x 35 x 8 feet. A large wooden impeller with an electric motor kept it liquefied. It then flowed through a pipe at the bottom corner, to be poured into horse drawn tank cars and used as fertilizer.

One day, the impeller broke at the bottom. The wooden sewage covers were taken off and the mechanism lifted out with ropes. In the meantime, the effluent continued into the septic container and for a while drained at the bottom through the pipe. As the mixture thickened, all hands lowered pails on ropes to reduce the sewage level. At about 5 feet down the pails could not be filled any more to make it worthwhile. Somebody had to go in, fill the pails and hand them up. The farmer told his two teenage sons to strip and get in there. Then he looked straight at me and said, "You would not dare to follow." He challenged me like an expert motivational pro and won. I am sure I would not have been fired if I had refused to climb into the sewer. It dawned on me later that I had a lot to learn.

A few weeks before Germany's surrender on May 8, 1945, the allied forces moved into Munich. All railroad and motorized traffic stood still including the main line from Munich to the Austrian border near Salzburg. A number of freight cars stood on sidings at the rural train station near the farm, one of them loaded with ammunition. We drove our truck to the station and to the siding closest to the open freight car full of potatoes and started to unload them with tines which is pretty awkward. We posted the farmer's teenager to keep an eye out for five dive bombers. They seemed to move unhurriedly from station to station, diving one by one, machine-gunning and dropping small 50 kg. bombs on switches or on anything else that moved.

We looked up and watched them occasionally but they had appeared to move off. At any rate, we had to get the potatoes home. The boy worked alongside but suddenly shouted and pointed up. The first of the two-engine U.S. bombers came diving down, aiming at our station. I took one leap off the potatoes, hit the ground, fell, got up and ran across the road next to the siding and behind a big old tree. The first plane down started with its two machine guns blasting at the freight cars, pulled up and banked as the second started its run.

I had noticed the rail car next to the one full of potatoes. I thought it might be better for me to move further away from the tree. After the second plane came through and pulled up, I ran into the open field at right angles to the station, to get as far away as possible from the car full of ammunition.

I stopped running and threw myself flat on the ground as the third plane lined up with the station. There was nothing else for me to do but to look straight up and watch this plane. It started firing its two machine guns and I clearly saw the plane veering off ever so slightly and instead aiming at me. It was bad enough to be so completely exposed but worse to hear the bullets hitting the ground all around me, machine-gunned so close to the end of the war.

Fortunately, this plane could not keep on this course for more than a few seconds and had to pull up. I waited until the fourth and fifth planes disappeared. The ammunition sitting at the siding did not explode, but the boy got hit by a bullet in his thigh and a very old farmer was hit through his cheeks as he sat on his wagon near the road without realizing what was happening. I tried to press on his carotid artery to reduce the bleeding but it didn't work because his skin was far too wrinkled and he died. We finally got the boy to a hospital in Rosenheim where he recovered soon after. Years later I saw him in his home in Tuntenhausen, his scar barely noticeable any more.

Now it was May 8, 1945 and Germany surrendered unconditionally. I was almost 22 years old and I had made it through 5 years of the war in good condition and spirit. I was alive where so many died or suffered cruelly. I had not been subjected to lengthy hardship. I was lucky.

All Germans in uniform were gathered by U.S. troops, marched to large fields or camps and imprisoned. At my place, civilians stood by on the side of the road as the remains of the German army marched past under guard to the Bad Aibling air field. They stayed there for some months, mostly in the open and with very little food. District farmers had collected a truck full of food, mostly bread and smoked meats, and wanted me to drive it into the camp. At the gate, I managed to say a few words in English and drive on into a hangar where a German senior officer organized the distribution.

It was a very beautiful spring in the foothills of the Alps where I worked close to Bad Aibling. In contrast to that, the population suffered as the Russian armies were moving through the Eastern countries and into Germany. Literally millions of German people tried to flee to the West. As the fighting stopped, they were forced to get out of what then became western Poland, and also out of other eastern communities. Next came the displaced persons of non-German origin who also had to be settled by the new regional German Government, mostly in temporary camps. With the cities partly destroyed in the now occupied remainder of Germany, any possible space left in homes, farms or public buildings was assigned by the local government to those without shelter. Food rationing was strictly enforced down to 750 calories per person per day.

In urban centers, the elderly found it very difficult to obtain their rations from small stores or from large kitchens. Streets, roads, buildings and bridges were only slowly repaired. All useable single bricks were cleaned up and reused. Water, gas and hydro became available again in Munich although with interruptions. Heating fuel remained difficult to obtain especially in the coming fall and winter months. The war came to an end but in many ways and for many people severe hardships continued or got still worse. It was the old and less able who could not continue to cope and just had to resign themselves. When I looked at their faces, I kept remembering that fate had dealt kinder with me. I managed to get into Munich occasionally with some supplies. Talking to people there and noticing the conditions in the summer of 1945, I was sure that I should continue to work at the farm in Tuntenhausen. So I stayed in that beautiful part of southern Bavaria and kept on working hard but at least with adequate food.

In the meantime, the U.S. Army began to establish small outposts in rural areas, usually in homes. These detachments controlled and checked whatever civilian traffic was allowed to move. A 9:00 p.m. curfew was enforced by heavily armed U.S. soldiers in mostly open Jeeps. Soon soldiers came to the farm and to my warehouse to get some potatoes, having everything else available from their quartermaster. They wanted to pay for them but I suggested that they exchange them instead for chocolate or some coffee, canned goods, or something like that. In return, I paid the farmer in cash for the potatoes. It took some time for him to wise up to the two-sided exchange.

In a small isolated clearing next to the farm, I discovered a number of abandoned staff cars in German army paint, among them a four-door 45 hp BMW cabriolet in reasonable condition, except for the left front window, and almost full of gas. The members of this small unit must have simply decided to take their uniforms off, put on civilian clothing and make their way home. What a priceless opportunity had come my way — to get my hands on a car. It was exciting enough just to start thinking of it as my own car! I collected as much gas as possible and drove it home to the farm, hiding it.

Now ownership papers had to be established. First, I called on the resident Catholic priest and explained to him the need for a second delivery vehicle to supply our bread to the grocery stores around the Bad Aibling area. On a piece of cardboard, I typed just the few words in English I knew, got the priest to sign and stamp it, then folded it into a plastic protector. Of course, this would not do for the German or American authorities but hopefully, at least for the time being, it would suffice within the local area. It did work and I drove my car a few times including through checkpoints where Americans had no trouble accepting my papers. This may have been due to them not really checking. They were invariably nice to me throughout the regular U.S. Army units stationed in Bavaria.

Getting overly confident, I decided to go for a trip close to the Austrian border at Salzburg. A co-worker promised to give me a new shirt if we would pick up his suitcase there. The second co-worker just wanted to come along for the ride. So off we went one fine Sunday morning in July, keeping on primary or secondary roads rather than using the nearby autobahn which I was sure would be kept for U.S. Army traffic. We made it successfully through several checkpoints and to the farm where we picked up the suitcase and got some supper as well.

It was now late afternoon when we started back, concerned about making it in good time to get home before the 9:00 p.m. curfew. I was driving through the sizeable village of Traunstein and was just about to congratulate myself on having made it through, when the brake fluid line broke. The handbrake had not worked at all. Garages were not open on Sundays and trying to stay overnight would be difficult and indeed not advisable. I had no choice but to get to the nearby autobahn, drive slowly, gear down and switch the ignition on and off. In this way it would be possible to slowly come to a complete stop if necessary. So I took my chances and off we went onto the autobahn toward Bad Aibling and home.

It seemed that there was no traffic whatsoever in my direction and very little in the other. The autobahn median was full of bushes quite close to the concrete pavement. A few kilometers ahead, the autobahn curved around a very hilly section, with one lane on the upper stretch going west with a retaining wall on the right. The other lane going east dropped down with the median angling quite steeply to the pavement.

Before we got to this retaining wall, the straight section was still without traffic so I felt quite good about the progress made. I should not have felt that way. From the side of the median a soldier stepped out, without his helmet or gun, waving one arm up and down. I found out later that this was a signal to slow down. My foot was off the gas pedal but I was going too fast to gear down. I looked into the mirror and as well told my rear passenger to keep turning around. He did but nobody seemed to follow, so I resumed speed. What I also did not know, but found out later, was that the military police Jeeps were souped up vehicles. All of a sudden, an open Jeep with three fully armed military police overtook and roared past me, turned into my lane and hit the brakes. I did not fully realize what happened but simply reacted to the red light flashing and them coming at me fast. I turned my steering wheel hard left, overtook and passed the Jeep, turned right into my lane, shifted into third and turned the ignition off, still going quite fast.

As far as the MPs were concerned, I was obviously trying to run away. The driver now turned left, back into the fast lane and drew up alongside me. The one sitting in the backseat drew his revolver and pointed it straight at me less than three feet away, shaking, yelling and shouting, "Stop! Stop! Stop!" My two passengers tried to crawl down under their seats but I could not. I had to face the gun and the incensed MP. I kept shouting, "Sorry, no brakes! Sorry, no brakes!" The situation became desperate. If it had not been for the MP sitting in front who turned and put his arm down on the one aiming to shoot, I could have been shot in the head. As it was, he and the driver on the left must have realized that a head shot at close range could have caused extensive damage to the Jeep and to them.

The driver now went ahead and passed me again, moved to the slow lane, touched the brakes and then slowed the Jeep as I shifted gears and turned the ignition off and on until both vehicles came to a complete stop. I stepped out on my side as fast as I could and leaned against my door as the driver came back to me, mumbling, "Sorry, no brakes. Sorry, no brakes."

He did not rough me up, perhaps because he could see that I was shaking at the knees.

To this day, I can see him in front of me, legs apart, one hand on his gun, the other pointing at my chest, saying very slowly, "You may continue but we could be on either side hiding, so you better stick to thirty miles per hour or you will be taken in." My companions picked themselves and the suitcase up and we drove on again, not without my telling them off for hiding and thereby provoking the MPs even more. The 9:00 p.m. curfew was now in effect and we almost made it home to the farm. However, a local German policeman stopped us. He looked at my papers, impounded the car and told us to walk home. As I did so, tired and saddened by the loss of my car, I realized that once again I had been very lucky. Perhaps I should tempt fate less frequently.

My work at the farm was increased as the fall season approached. All help was out in the field working past sundown stacking hay with pitchforks, following on either side of the horse-drawn wagon. The farmer had a 125 cc motorbike and with field glasses, looking from the top of the farm buildings, would check on our progress. Once, he came across the field with his bike, put it down close to where I worked, took my fork and started to pick up hay, hoist it up to the wagon and repeat the motion several times while practically skipping alongside. Then he handed the fork back to me in the manner of an instructor, saying , "This is the way for you to do it." Then he picked up his bike and left. All I could do was just stand there with my mouth wide open for some time.

Then seed cleaning started in my warehouse for sunflower and rye. Although all windows were wide open, heavy dust and blowing air could not be avoided in this type of operation. I did not have any masks but tried to put moist pieces of cloth over my mouth. I got a really bad cold and could not get rid of a persistent heavy cough. As much as I appreciated eating enough and getting some food occasionally into Munich, I could not afford to get really sick so I said goodbye to a real work experience and went back to Munich.

7

WORKING FOR THE U.S. ARMY

Returning to Munich was quite a shock. I now saw more of the city and for the first time it looked permanently damaged with obvious signs of make-shift repairs. Most of the rubble blocking the streets was removed. Water, gas and hydro lines were restored, the last two often interrupted to save fuel. Food distribution worked reasonably well except for the frequent lack of some items. All of them were strictly rationed, needing coupons even in restaurants. Buildings were inadequately or not heated at all. For example, apartment staircases were unheated and lit only with 12 second automatic timers to conserve hydro. Everybody huddled in one room and were lucky to have some source of heating. Munich can be quite damp and miserable in the fall and winter as it was in 1945/46.

It was depressing enough to note the appearance of the city but even more so the depression in the faces of the people. I could see that most of them were worn out and worried, especially the older ones. The young ones could fend for themselves but even they found it difficult to try and accomplish something in their lives. There were no real signs of improvement. Germany was truncated. The remaining four parts were cut into allied sections. The cities and industries were severely damaged and reparations were insisted on by the Russians. The German Reichsmark was still the medium of exchange for official purposes only. Almost all goods and services were exchanged by bartering. As a result, practically everything could be obtained on the black market and money lost almost all of its value.

Under these conditions, I became quite discouraged. Now I had to get used to eating very little. Being hungry for a few hours or days can be overcome. If the lack of food persists, at least in my experience, it undermines the brain and I was inclined to be unreasonable. To say it in the simplest way is to say that I felt like a dog, with only one thing in mind - to get food. I also experienced a strong resentment against all others who were fed well, had nice clothes and obviously good soap, such as the U.S. military and civilians, all of whom were very well looked after in contrast to most of us.

I did not even try to study; most universities had not opened yet. To get a job in the civilian food supply system did not make sense to me. It was obvious that the only job worth getting was with the U.S. Occupation. This is what I did and found a job with plenty of food, unfortunately not without conditions. I became an inventory clerk. The U.S. Army Quartermaster Corps had established a huge depot at the north end of Munich, partly on open ground and partly in warehouses, with enough food stacked there for a six month period. Displaced Polish men in partly U.S. uniforms and with guns patrolled the compound inside and out, including the gate. The German workers leaving at night were spot-checked and if caught with pilfered items got an automatic three-month jail term. In spite of that, every so often a worker would tempt the odds and put some coffee into his hollowed-out heels or books. A slightly better and less risky method was to stay inside a warehouse as often and as long as possible, open cans of condensed milk and add ice cream powder to it which was very nourishing.

Outside, cartons full of k-rations, pre-packaged iron rations, were more challenging. These cartons were stored on level ground in stacks about 10 x 10 x 10 feet. Of course it was not necessary to count the length, width and height of a stack or to count the top layers. However, two of us persuaded the Polish guard that this was necessary because the top layer might contain uneven or odd numbers of cartons. More often than not, the guards were too lazy to climb up the ladder but did keep an eye on us. One of us would climb up and measure, count and write very slowly, constantly keeping near the top edges in sight of the guard. The other would cut the strap, tear open the carton, take out the k-ration, put the carton back upside down and reattach the loose metal straps on the carton. This procedure was indeed very fast and if the guard made a move to climb up to the edge, we would report right away that evidently some pilfering had occurred.

It did not take long for me to realize the precarious aspect of my job and the chance of not being able to continue university studies at some point in the future because of a jail term. So I resigned with a mixture of relief and regret for the missing food and became a driver. U.S. Army vehicles were assigned to German drivers to make it unnecessary to use U.S. drivers. It was possible for me to come up with some food so I could give my German ration card to my mother. I also could have a means of transportation and I loved to drive Jeeps.

There were a number of interesting trips during that time. Right after the surrender in May, 1945 the U.S. Army authority established a censorship division, also in Munich. The members were emigrants recruited in the United States, speaking fluent German, were mostly Jewish, given army uniforms without rank or insignia and called U.S. civilians.

One of them was given the weekly assignment to drive and call on every German post office in the State of Bavaria. He was to walk in unexpected, order the employees to take an empty large canvas bag and fill it with whatever letters or parcels happened to be about, seal the bag and order for it to be sent to Munich by post. There the contents were opened and examined, but I could never find out beyond that whether anything was ever done about them.

My U.S. civilian liked being driven as much as I liked driving. We started our weekly tour in Munich to come home on Saturdays but I persuaded him to work faster. As a result, we detoured around Stuttgart once and several times past Munich into Salzburg which of course was highly irregular. At each of the last post office calls for the day, we would look up the resident army detachment officer for U.S. civilians to stay the night. Most of the time, he would make it possible for me to sleep there as well and even to eat there too. This was truly appreciated especially in view of the fact that he was Jewish and had just recently emigrated to the U.S. with his German parents.

In the Spring of 1946, I must have been one of the very few German civilians who could travel every week all over the State of Bavaria. At first hand, I could see what had been done to so many beautiful cities. I could not help but look at them and the people there, knowing that they had no chance to rebuild. Before that, monetary and financial incentives would have to be instituted and the occupation authorities ready and willing to remove the heavy burden on Germany.

There was one particular driving assignment which then, and even now, I find difficult to think about. For several weeks in 1946, I was chosen to drive a high-ranking U.S. Army officer on several trips, with a three-quarter ton open army truck which was clumsy and difficult to drive. Unlike U.S. staff officers who would sit next to the driver, this one sat in the rear just like German officers used to do. The only explanation I could find was that he did not want to sit next to a German. Perhaps there was a reason.

Let me digress. On December 17, 1944, the Ardennes Campaign, also called the Battle of the Bulge, took place outside a little place called Malbedy in Belgium. A unit of the German 1st Panzer Division of the SS, 150th brigade, in heavy fighting overran a U.S. unit of the 285th Battalion, Battery B. About 150 prisoners of war were taken; 80 were killed, 70 survived. As a result of this atrocity, the U.S. 328th infantry regiment then issued a written order to the effect that "no SS troops or paratroopers will be taken as prisoners of war but will be shot on sight". Without any question, this order resulted in uncounted atrocities against German and U.S. POWs as the war continued unabated.

About a year later, 73 former members of this SS unit were tried by a U.S. military tribunal at Dachau, near Munich. 43 were sentenced to death, 22 given sentences of 8 to 10 year prison terms. Some terms were subsequently commuted, largely due to U.S. Senator McCarthy and other senators who toured U.S. Army installations in Germany in 1946. He spoke out against this tribunal causing it to commute and prevent more hangings. For some, it was too late; they had been hanged in Landsberg shortly thereafter.

The Lieutenant Colonel, whom I was driving, was the commanding officer of Battery B, the members of which were captured on December 17, 1944. He attended the military tribunal several times and I sat in the court room waiting.

Only a few feet separated me from the benches on which the former German soldiers sat. I looked at them and they looked back at me. I thought about what must have gone on in their minds, in their utter helplessness and their inevitable death. I had to leave the tribunal and the courtroom, thinking of and quoting John Bradford, the English Protestant martyr, "There but for the grace of God go I."

I just could not remain in the tribunal. I started to walk around outside but kept in sight of the court building. There was not much to see here of the former concentration camp, its wooden buildings and barracks. In the centre of the administration, I found what turned out to be a two-unit crematorium but no gas chamber. The gate still showed a large sign on top: Arbeit Macht Frei -Work Will Set You Free. I picked up the Colonel and with a heavy heart drove him through the gate, the victorious soldier being free, the condemned vanquished and in chains.

Quite some time later, I was told that there had been about 50,000 inmates in Dachau. I had known it existed and I had seen some of them in Munich helping to remove unexploded bombs. Afterwards, people would come up with some food, as little as they had, and hand it to the inmates, the guards helping. I knew of this concentration camp then, but not of any others until later. At a co-worker's wedding in 1943, I asked the SS groom what he was doing in Dachau. He said he had just been decorated for bravery, then assigned to Dachau and had been told there not to discuss details.

The officers of the military tribunal were quartered in a home in Garmisch-Partenkirchen that belonged to a German industrialist and had been taken over. I drove the Colonel from Munich to this place several times. In one case, we arrived there late for a full-fledged party. I stayed in the kitchen helping myself to some food, listening to the drunken proceedings. I could make out some words over the shouting and laughter. Evidently, somebody joked about a prosecutor and a witness and everybody thought it hilarious. Perhaps the mocking witness actually saw an SS soldier murdering someone and repeated it being drunk, or maybe he just made it up for the edification of his buddies. Of course I will never know, but I will always remember the incident. I did not continue working for the motor pool.

By chance, I found a job combining driving and, on weekends, sailing, believe it or not. I happened to be on the shore of Lake Starnberg, 25 kilometers south of Munich, noticing some larger sailboats. A local standing beside me said that of course, it was the Americans who had taken these boats and one officer was looking for a guide. It appeared that he was the local officer of the then called CIC, Counter Intelligence Corps. He hired me on the spot without checking any of the fake references I had mentioned. I did not know how to sail but pretended I did. Neither did he. I was supposed to pick up the beautiful 40 foot racer that was being checked over and in a few days sail it to its buoy about one kilometer away, south of Starnberg.

I went back to Munich immediately and got a library book on how to learn to sail. I just barely made it by myself to the buoy, helped by very little wind and by pushing around the boom by hand while every so often looking at the book for what to do next. Fortunately, nobody observed this and I eventually made it to the estate of the Countess von Blucher, nee von Siemens, both names of an illustrious German lineage. E. W. von Siemens was a 19th century manufacturer, inventor and pioneer. Marshal von Blucher was with England's Duke of

Wellington in the Battle of Waterloo defeating Napoleon in 1815. The young Count was killed during the war. The officers of the CIC and their help took over the estate and the Countess together with two retainers were moved into the coach house. One German driver shared an attic room with me. It was quite a set up. There were six officers in the house, one Lieutenant Colonel commanding this unit, one major, one captain, two lieutenants and occasionally some guests. The German help consisted of one professional German chef, one butler, four maids, the driver and me.

There was no dinghy so I swam out to the buoy every day claiming I had to get the boat ready. I also had to bring along my instruction book covered in plastic. The first attempts were deplorable but my guests had not sailed before either. I became reasonably proficient which included getting the boat back to its buoy with 16 people on board after a severe storm in July, 1946. This was very much appreciated, but a disaster could have happened considering there were no life vests on board, something I had not thought of.

I was pleased with my employment and my employers were pleased with me. After the storm, some of them talked nicely to me while sailing or being driven on their various assignments. I started to realize that they were very much Americans in that they were inclined to be easygoing, straight forward and unpretentious which was in contrast to many Germans. I was interested in getting to know them but could not go beyond a certain point. I was still not able to understand or speak English except for very short sentences. This was annoying. I felt like a dolt and wanted to change that.

By chance I saw a book titled *One Thousand Words of English* by Tousaint-Langescheid, divided into commonly used expressions, and some explanation of grammar. Working and living in a rural setting meant I had to study with this book on my own. Memorizing simple English words did not seem to result in speaking, so I made up short meaningful sentences. I wrote them down on foolscap which I folded lengthwise with German on the left and English on the right.   I memorized about 10 complete sentences per lesson. Every time I started again at night, I would review and note which one was not instantly recalled, then repeated that again if necessary until perfect. I started every night at 8:00 p.m. and continued until midnight.

The complete book indicated that about five months would result in speaking simple but correct English including the prerequisite grammar and spelling. I had decided in three months that I could handle about 1,200 complete, meaningful sentences correctly. To provide some fun, I kept speaking my broken English for everybody around. My English quickly got better but it was hard work every evening and Sundays—no movies in Starnberg and no girlfriends either.

Halfway towards my goal, as the light kept annoying the other driver in my room, the Lieutenant in the next attic room came in one night and found out what I was doing. He wanted to know how I would be able to pronounce sentences correctly on my own. He suggested that I come over and he would help me. I had to repeat everything until he was satisfied and he promised not to say anything to the other officers. As a result, for quite a few years, I kept having a very slight Boston accent.

It had not been without a great deal of frustration and constant repetition but the sweet moment of success arrived. Three months to the day, I went half-way down the spiral staircase to the hall, stood and gazed at the officers assembled there that morning before leaving for their assignments. When all of them looked up at me wondering, I addressed them in correct and fluent English, wishing them a good morning, having had a restful night, hoping for good weather and a very pleasant day for everyone, etc. To this day, I can hear in my mind my first English speech and see their completely dumbfounded expressions.

There was a sequel to all of this. The Captain wanted to know how on earth I would keep on improving my grammar and suggested that I find a retired school teacher. On telling him that I could find one in Starnberg, he let me use his personal car twice a week for lessons there. Next, the Major handling the estate fired the butler and decided that I could do it instead just as well, in addition to my sailing. He instructed me in all details, for example, to stand two inches behind and left of the Colonel at dinner, how the girls would serve without any talking, only guided by looks given by me. I served wine to the Colonel only, with an immaculate serviette over my lower left arm, attired in my good dark suit.

It was quite a job. The large kitchen was downstairs with a dumb waiter up to the pantry and into the main dining room. As the food was brought up, sometimes I hid part of the first entree for myself instead of taking it to the dining room. The chef had his suspicions and would come running up the stairs as the dumb waiter moved up, but he never caught me. After breakfast, the girls had to do the bedrooms. As instructed, I put on white gloves and with one of the girls with me, I went over the bureaus and other wood furniture to check for dust. I would just turn my glove over and show her without comment by either of us. The officers at the Countess von Blucher Estate by now were used to my speaking fluent English. They asked questions and I answered in proper

English. They let me become as outspoken as they were, which made for interesting exchanges of German and American views, especially on pre-war German history.

I had an interesting job and was living very well indeed. I heard very little German spoken and was not constantly reminded of the absolute poverty in my torn-apart country. In 1946, an international conference demanded 20 billion U.S. dollars in reparations. If it had not been for the increasing trouble with Russia, more Germans could have perished and died after the war than during the war. As it happened, in 1946 some attempts were made to lessen the unbelievable economic and social misery in the American and British zones, not to speak of the Russian zone.

In 1947, the Americans finally realized that all of Europe and especially western Germany would have to be given substantial supplies on credit, to be paid back eventually. This was announced in the Marshall Plan of June, 1947. After that, the German economy was still stagnant because of the huge amount of printed German money which had accumulated for many years.

The occupation powers intended to do something about this inflation but only to keep in force regulations and all American and English economic governmental planning. On June 20, 1948, German Zonal Minister Ludwig Erhard, who was in charge of German currency reform, simply threw out all of the governmental decrees and regulations. This he did on his own initiative and against orders. This was a very brave and far-reaching example of civil courage. At the stroke of midnight June 20, 1948, all currency, coins, paper, deposits and credit were decreed worthless. Whatever used to be called Reichsmark was declared useless. Instead, every German could get 40 new Deutschmarks in cash. Some old money still in banks could be exchanged for new on a percentage basis for existing payrolls or for goods and services if approved. Other values such as mortgages were re-evaluated as well. Within hours, the existing equity of all Germans was enormously reduced. What had taken many years since 1918 of effort and savings was gone. The only thing for Germany to do was to start again. I had not seen all of what was coming but I certainly saw the results, starting the very next day. Everybody who could possibly work did, and kept working. Anyone having any goods or services offered them for sale. The black market dried up and disappeared; pent-up production followed consumption and created wealth. West Germany literally arose from apathy and the country rebuilt itself with a vengeance. Working took over — "Furor Teutonicus".

8

STUDYING IN GERMANY AND THE U.S.A.

In 1948, I started a new job with a chance of getting into management, promotions and higher pay, but first I had to start at the bottom as a warehouse stock boy in the U.S. Post Exchange system. Shortly thereafter, I became an assistant manager of a small branch at the time that the currency conversion took place in 1948. From then on, I was paid very well and now had a chance to save the "new" money, but I did not have enough to go back to university on a full-time basis. That took another year.

In the early summer of 1949, I felt I could study without also having to work and as well give some support to my mother. I had become an assistant manager of two combined large post exchanges with over 100 German employees. I had a car and an interesting job, living very well indeed. It was tempting to stay where I was but I kept in mind that my educational back-ground was sketchy and certainly not in line with professional demands. To a certain extent, I had achieved some success in studying, obtaining the special high school diploma but I was exceptionally well coached then by my mother and my cousin, Lore. Also, I had achieved some success in speaking proper English. What was ahead, however, would be a different and daunting academic challenge.

I would have to improve my German, learn to concentrate, listen, read, retain and then recall thoughts in logical sequence in an academic setting. In the last five years, I had done very little of this. I had not been able to earn some of the credits of the 1943/44 semesters. These missing subjects had to be taken first before proceeding which meant a double load of courses. To make up for lost time and get my degree in the shortest possible time, I had to go to unusual lengths. For one, I had met the girl I wanted to marry but not before graduation. I never did like the aspect of something half finished. Gusti Schmeckenbecher and I met in 1948 when she ran the office at the U.S. Post Exchange System on the army base in Bad Tolz where I had just been promoted Assistant Manager. During this year we worked closely together, were impressed by each other and wanted to stay together.

There was another reason for me to take a very heavy lecture load. I had seen an advertisement on the university bulletin board announcing a one-year scholarship to the United States. This included travel expenses, tuition and living allowance for one full year, upon application and competitive selection. I remember having turned away from the board thinking it was too good to be possible. Far too many students would apply and only a few could succeed. My friend and colleague suggested I should try anyway. So I did and got the scholarship after almost a full year and four interviews later. As the 1949/50 interviews progressed and I was still in the running and seemed to have a chance after all, I found it difficult at times to keep studying. Occasionally, I veered off from the straight and narrow, dreaming of America, its vastness and beautiful landscape. I had seen maps and pictures but I could not really imagine that I might get there one day. Imagining was pointless. It would be a long time before Germans would be allowed to travel. It looked like the victors of the war wanted to keep all Germans down. Except for political and global expediency some improvements were allowed in 1947, starting with the Marshall Plan, and again in 1948, with the currency reform. Then West Germany started to literally rise from the ashes and I wanted to be part of it. But to travel abroad would be a long time in coming for anybody.

It was time to work out an approach to getting my degree. How could I get the impossible number of lecture hours onto my proposed timetable every week? It just could not be done unless there was another student involved. Fortunately, I met a colleague, Gerhard Vatke, and we became friends. He was going through for the same degree, with the same number of courses and for the same graduation year. So we decided to try and co-operate. He would sit in on lecture 'A' and I on 'B'. At night, he would present subject 'A' to me but in a very concentrated way and for only 1/2 hour, and then I would present subject 'B' to him also in 1/2 hour, coaching each other constantly. We became very proficient at this, in effect covering several different lectures per night for each of us, getting the degree in much less time.

In order to get enough sleep to keep this up, I rented a small bedroom in a house directly across from the university, much as I had read about U.S. flophouse-beds rented by the hour. There, usually alternately, we slept between lectures or tutorials, sometimes for less than one hour at a time. We learned to study effectively. In addition, my mother helped us in every way, providing sandwiches and coffee, leaving us undisturbed at night, month after month as we studied. Neither one of us could have succeeded without her help.

The months passed quickly as graduation approached. My friend felt that in order to be on the safe side, he would go on for one more year. I thought I should go ahead and take the exams. I did not feel reasonably prepared but made the decision to go for it. Part of that reason was the announcement that I had been selected for the scholarship. The other reason was the understanding Gusti and I had to be married upon graduation.

Munich University allowed students to sit in and listen to oral examinations. For two weeks, my friend sat right behind me and knew very well how I sweated. Then it was over and I had made it after a great deal of determination, effort and luck. I kept reminding myself that I was now an academic, but should keep in mind the proviso that I lacked a complete senior matriculation. I now spoke English well, and I graduated from Munich University proud, elated and, I must admit, pleased with myself. I was studying in 1943/44 for one year with increasing interruptions, and for a full year in 1949/50. Normally at least three full years were required for this degree. Having done it in two must have resulted in some damage to myself. Unceasing mental concentration for one year together with prolonged absence of any relaxation almost made me feel like a zombie. I have come close to that again in some later years, fanatically determined to succeed without considering alternatives, to overdo things at times. I found out that success breeds success and does more for you than most anything else, but it should not be overdone.

In mid-July, 1950 I got married, and one week later I left by train for Cannes and boarded a ship bound for New York via Lisbon and the Azores. On the boat, I became ill for a few days, probably in reaction to the mental strain of the last year. I was quite listless for some time and could not take in all the scenery. I went over the experience of the past months and only slowly could I turn away from it toward the new and exciting images of what was lying ahead of me.

Finally, early in the morning as the sun rose and the fog began to lift, the Statue of Liberty and the buildings of Manhattan came into view, just as seen in the movies but now really seen by me, standing on a ship, feeling it vibrate, hearing distant sounds and smelling the salt air. All of this was in my mind and still is. I can recall it at any time even after these many years, except perhaps for sniffing the strong salt air. As one gets older one cannot recall smells as easily any more.

Almost two weeks were spent sightseeing in Manhattan, mostly on foot and with a hole in one shoe, but I never tired of taking in the buildings, the traffic and the people. There is no other city like New York and there was no comparison to Munich. One could say that even the older buildings were new, and the new ones were very different. Trying to look up at skyscrapers left me dizzy. As to the people of New York, I noticed many different types and hues from mostly European origins. I realized what was really meant by the American melting pot which created these tall buildings. Somehow I imagined that they put a touch on the inhabitants. I was simply overwhelmed by Manhattan.

Quite often, when talking to Americans or reading, I missed typical expressions, phrases or slang. To prevent losing out on them, I started to look up current and back issues of Time and kept this up. Also, I was fortunate to be able to understand the Manhattan accent. On top of the Empire State Building, I met a family from South Dakota. They invited me to a Chinese dinner when they found out that I was going to Lincoln, Nebraska. Their farm had to be looked after by a small airplane, it was that big. Later I learned that there are only two types of Chinese restaurants, first rate and mostly others. This family evidently worked and lived on a scale then completely beyond my comprehension. Yet they were without airs or boasts. They were simply themselves. When later I got to Lincoln, Nebraska, I met more westerners like them.

As the train travelled west toward Chicago, I kept looking at the beautiful Allegheny Mountains but did not notice any specific towns or cities. I simply must have been exhausted. In Chicago, somebody must have taken a photo of me but all I remember was a skyscraper. I have no recollection of staying overnight or of starting for Nebraska and Lincoln. I do recall sitting in a very comfortable coach for the some eight-hundred miles and noticing the landscape gradually turning into prairie. I felt the staccato rhythm of the rails which had not yet been welded lengthwise, hearing the drawn-out plaintive whistle so very different from a high-pitched German locomotive, and listening to the sound of approaching and receding rural crossings. These sounds put me to sleep or woke me up and in my mind, the memories of the days and weeks crowded in on me and were packed so tightly that I could not differentiate between them. The bit of railroading I had done in the past, including the one without tickets, was totally different from this one, going into the heartland of the United States. I slept comfortably, waking somewhat refreshed and looking forward to another interesting day.

A beautiful sunny morning in September, 1950 greeted me in Lincoln as I stepped off the train. My first impression was of the huge grain elevators on sidings, the incredible blueness of the sky and the noticeable dryness in the air causing my nose to twitch. Later, there were many more days like this. Lincoln is on about the same latitude as Rome but very different, being in the middle of the continent. A long journey was behind me. How could I not be refreshed on a day like this? As I walked down the main street to the YMCA, I encountered a parade led by majorettes in very short skirts and boots. I was welcomed to Lincoln.

Next morning, I asked how long it would take to get to the foothills of Colorado, to visit a former girlfriend who had married an American soldier, both now farming there. I then called at the University to register but was told that this would not take place for another week. So I thought it would be nice to visit my friend and see that part of Colorado. I had enough monthly allowance money and could take a bus, but with this beautiful early fall weather, hitchhiking would be good for getting in shape and would let me fully experience the prairie. So, early the next morning I was on the road and started most certainly to experience all of it and then some. Interstate highways going east-west and north-south were not in place yet and major roads connected all of the larger towns. I followed the main road due west just like the pioneers in their wagons, and I must say that I did not think I could proceed any much faster. I was picked up quite frequently but also dropped off at north-south intersections going to smaller places and left there to wait for another ride. I would start to walk because I thought I had a better chance of being picked up. Instead of standing still or hunkering down, there being very few fence posts, I ended up walking in early morning, through high noon and into late afternoons. I met real farmers mostly in older cars and all were open and friendly. I recall one old farmer who had only one place for me to sit which was on his toolbox. More often than not politics was discussed. He was totally against the late President Roosevelt. For several hours I had to sit up straight, learning about his war years before the farmer finally had to turn off.

After three days, I finally made it close to the Colorado foothills and took a bus the rest of the way. I had a great opportunity to take in and remember a part of this fabulous land that seemed to go on forever and ever. I learned a great deal on this trip, one of which was never again to hitchhike for nearly 600 miles.

My friends took me by car to the top of Colorado's Pikes Peak. At 14,000 feet, I looked out into the distant Rocky Mountains, very short of breath. On the left and right going down the road, you realized that beyond fifty feet on either side nothing could be seen other than the rock formations - true wilderness. This is very much in contrast with the Alps where some sign of human endeavor is always noticeable.

I do not remember much of the farm or its buildings. I was glad to take a bus back into Lincoln, falling asleep off and on, or looking out the bus window into the bright hot sunshine, or watching people get in or out at the bus stops, or just daydreaming about what I had seen. Back in Lincoln, it was high time to organize the school year.

First, I rented a room close to the university. It was a typical wooden two-bedroom house owned by a railroad conductor whom I rarely met, and his wife who was out most of the time, an ideal place to study. Next, I found another ideal part-time job in the cloakroom at the YWCA. I could also eat supper there, all of which did not interfere much with studying. Supermarkets had not yet come to Lincoln but I found a grocery store for some supplies and met the owner. Without hesitation, he handed over his car key and told me to explore the surroundings of Lincoln by myself. Granted that cars were commonplace there, he did not even find out if I could drive. It was typical of the friendliness shown to a stranger. A German would at least have gone along or done the driving.

The first graduate year of 1950 started in September. My faculty adviser accepted my records and allowed me to proceed to a Masters Degree in only one graduate year instead of the required and usual two. I had looked closely at all the required reading and tutorials, as well as an outline of a proposed thesis, but of course to be written in English. Compared to what I had done in Munich, I thought I had a chance to do the Masters Degree in only one year so I proceeded to fill in my timetable with the courage of my convictions. After all, with only a one-year scholarship, I wanted to get the advanced degree, a real challenge.

Now starting in 1950 in Lincoln, I studied as determinedly as a year ago in Munich but this time in English. I did not have my friend and colleague at my side now or assistance from my mother. This time, I was completely on my own. I made certain to side step all invitations and spent all my waking hours at the library, at home or in the cloakroom of the YWCA. The cloakroom, fortunately, was not busy often and eating there took very little time. Having learned how to learn, I could move through some assignments quickly and retained material well. My command of English improved accordingly but I did not realize the difficulty of expressing involved concepts or specialized terms in economic writing.

The idea of proposing a thesis in English started to loom larger in my consciousness one evening. As I sat at my desk alone in the house working through these problems, I considered writing a thesis in German first and then translating it. This of course had to be dismissed immediately, the reason being that I might as well think I could translate German poetry into the equivalent English. So I was forced to get back to writing in English. There was no alternative.

I think I can say that I have not been emotional very often except perhaps at Christmas time. In complete frustration, I got up from my desk and stood at my dresser. I felt sorry for myself and very alone. Then I looked at myself in the mirror in utter despair. At that moment, I began to weep, tears streaming down my cheeks, suddenly realizing this. At first, I was totally taken aback by this performance and made a desperate effort to stop sobbing convulsively but could not. I was in the grip of an over-powering force. I could not help myself. Years later, whenever anyone claimed to not be able to help themselves, I thought perhaps that person may also have had some true and sufficient reason to feel that way after all.

I then let go of the dresser and threw myself on my bed. The sobbing and shaking continued. I could not calm down or in any way perceive what was going on. I was out of my mind. I became utterly exhausted but before becoming unconscious, I must have been aware of my shoes on my bed, something which I never do. With a real effort, I wanted to take them off but could not move at all.

Late the next morning I came to, still completely dazed and exhausted. It certainly was a frightening experience. I never read about it except in history where Otto von Bismark is said to have suffered a "weinkrampf", evidently similar to my nervous breakdown. I do not know what he did about it but I took immediate steps to avoid a repeat performance. It did not occur to me to see a doctor. I would handle this myself.

First, together with my graduate student adviser, I abandoned the attempt to write a thesis and changed courses so that they would lead to only a one-year graduate course. I would have to go through a second year after the scholarship year in order to get a Masters Degree. This, of course, immediately resulted in my feeling and living better as well as beginning to take part in other activities. I actually read books again, other than text books, and started to accept invitations to things on weekends and short trips with friends. For the first time in my life, I could be a student doing things that they have always done.

Before that, however, I wanted to do something which had been neglected for quite some time. My upper teeth had deteriorated badly ever since Russia. The dentist in Lincoln strongly and rather enthusiastically proposed to go all the way and recess my gums as well. All of my teeth would have to go anyway and I would become more handsome. I must say that I did not like the most annoying cracking sounds made in my head but at least it didn't hurt much.

I enjoyed my newly found ease to study but could not forget the nervous breakdown that had taken place so devastatingly. Something had to be done to prevent a recurrence, something that would increase my will power and mental stamina. I thought I had done well on both accounts but obviously would have to do better.

I had gone to the library and noticed a self-help book, *How to Hypnotize Yourself*. I glanced at it and thought that it seemed like something that would make me improve on a number of shortcomings. Evidently, you could go through the chapters and arrive at the point of issuing short commands to yourself to do or not to do something inside your body. I had not yet heard much of Yoga except in a dictionary but it seemed that similar suggestions were made. As to hypnosis, I was not interested in applying it to other people. I wanted to get the better of myself and improve.

It was obvious that the suggested exercises would demand a great deal of time and above all utmost concentration. I went home and as usual was alone. I started chapter one of the exercises. I stretched out on my back, hands at my sides, palms down, at ease, with eyes closed, trying not to think at all. Now I started to concentrate only on my left hand up to the wrist, as long as it would take to lose all feeling and awareness in the hand. This is then repeated for the arm to the elbow and arm to shoulder. After quite a number of repetitions, I could start off with the complete left arm and instantly put it away. Going on in the same sequence to the right arm, I could put it away as well in one command. It took several weeks of working on these exercises every night for hours at a time, with both legs in the same sequence. Finally the body members and the torso were told in one word to relax, all sensation gone except for a much lower heartbeat and a less heavy head. In one moment, I was aware of being on my bed; in the next moment, I had left my consciousness. I could set a time for re-appearance just like a clock or simply change into normal sleep. It was truly uncanny. I did better in what I tried to accomplish. Later on, I got largely away from consistent self-hypnosis. The enormous effort of will to repeat single-mindedly a mantra to this extent was too much.

9

IMMIGRATION TO CANADA

At the end of 1950 and the beginning of 1951, the fighting in South Korea with the United States escalated. It could be considered possible at that time that Russia and therefore Europe might become involved, including Germany. Having been close to a war, it seemed that a better place to live would be on this side of the Atlantic. I could not remain in the States without first having to go back to Germany and applying for immigration, the same as for other countries and nationalities.

I went by bus to see the Canadian Consulate in Chicago but no exception could be made there. So I decided to apply for immigration later on, after arriving in Canada, and wrote to Gusti, my wife, telling her to apply immediately in Germany for immigration to Canada. Once she had arrived there as a landed immigrant, I was confident that as the husband, I could stay and apply there.

The end of the school year arrived and I passed all requirements in good standing. Then I received a letter from Gusti that her Canadian immigration papers had been approved and that she would expect to arrive in Toronto via Halifax some time at the end of June, 1951. I had about four more weeks to go before meeting her there.

My scholarship allowance of $72 a month had always been adequate. I managed to save some of it which I added to the money I made from the YWCA job. That would still not be enough to get to Toronto and I did not want to risk hitchhiking. While I was looking around for a job, the grocery store owner who befriended me in the fall told me about a brickyard outside of Lincoln. I went there and was hired on an hourly incentive basis to load bricks into wheelbarrows and into a kiln, or remove and stack them in the yard after they had been fired. This was done by teams of workers who were paid by the number of fired kilns per team. The boys relied on a constant high output of soft bricks placed into kilns and fired bricks removed from kilns, and on the tearing down and bricking up of kilns, of which there were 16 in double rows, going up and down the line as the kilns slowly "cooked" the bricks.

In June, it was still raining sometimes. Then narrow boards were put down crisscrossing to the kilns, to the brick-forming shed and to the brickyard. With heavily loaded brick wheelbarrows, the boys were able to move fast on these boards and change directions without letting a wheel touch down into the mud. I was not able to do that and more than once spilled the load and had to re-stack the bricks. Until then, I thought I was pretty good at balancing and co-ordination. It is amazing how all of a sudden one comes up against a new experience after many years of certainty.

The foreman could not let the boys make less money because of me. He gave me a normal weekly rate enabling me to earn more money than I could have made anywhere else. Now I was given the job of opening up kilns and with the boys taking out finished bricks and putting soft ones back in. Then

I would start mortaring bricks and closing the kiln. I barely kept up with the team as we followed kiln after kiln.

I survived and was happy to have made enough money at the brickyard. Now I can appreciate the hard work involved. I can also recall the smell of bad french fries coming from the diner as I waited at 5:30 in the mornings to be picked up by a co-worker. He was the one who found out that I could get a free ride by semi-trailer from Lincoln to Chicago. I had hitchhiked in the mid-west, rode a bus back from Colorado, studied, worked and made friends. I was truly enriched by all that had happened. Now a new experience and a new country beckoned. I still had the courage of my convictions and about $95 in my pocket, after having pre-paid for a bus ticket from Chicago to Detroit and a train ticket to Toronto.

I had also pre-paid and sent off all my books and other belongings care of Union Station, Toronto except for one small briefcase. The idea was for me to cross the border at Detroit into Canada as a tourist. The first trouble came at the U.S. line when an officer wanted to see my draft paper because of the Korean situation. I convinced him that I was a foreign student and he let me pass. I then expected some difficulty with the officer at the Canadian side but I simply kept going past him. He must have assumed I was a day-time tourist. At any rate I had landed in Canada but not as an immigrant.

I had sent a letter to Munich saying that I would try to get to Toronto at the end of June. Gusti would arrive by immigrant boat and train around the same time and would wait for me at Union Station's arrival area. If I was late for one day and did not show up, she was to find a place and I would inquire at the lost and found booth for her whereabouts. I boarded the first train at Windsor for Toronto, arriving only a few hours later than she had from Halifax via Montreal, and found her sitting on a bench in the arrival concourse of Toronto's Union Station. She had about $150 U.S. and I had a little over $50. Now we were set to take on the new country together.

Toronto was the choice for us to settle in Canada. We had read very little about it, still less about Montreal or Vancouver. Except for greetings, neither of us spoke French and the west coast was like another continent away. We felt we could better our chances at employment right in Toronto so we started looking for a job the very next morning. So far, signs and portents seemed to go our way. We could not possibly have expected to meet each other in Toronto, at the train station on a given day, time and place, or to have had such a plan worked out in Munich several weeks ahead. However, this is exactly what happened and luck stayed with us in the following days.

We had found a cheap rooming house at 12 McGill Street, close to downtown. Early Monday morning we went to the immigration office and Gusti presented her papers. After they were processed and accepted, the officer turned to me and wanted to know who I was. When I told him I was her husband and had just arrived from Lincoln, Nebraska, without any papers, he asked me a few questions. He then decided on the spot to let me stay in the country and to start immigration procedures forthwith. However, to become a citizen took until August 15, 1958. Thanks to his decision, we could legally be together in Canada. After this, the immigration officer then continued to do even more for us.

Gusti had thought of finding some secretarial work and I wanted to do my second graduate year in order to obtain my

Masters Degree. How could this be done? How and when would we be able to raise the two hundred dollar tuition fee? This immigration officer had an idea and made a phone call.

The next instant, we found ourselves in a taxi on our way to meet Mrs. Webb. We were interviewed and hired as a domestic couple for the months of July and August, 1951 for altogether, $200.00. This settled, we met Mr. Webb, stored Gusti's belongings at McGill Street and were in his car on our way to a large stone-house cottage, near McCrachen Landing, Stoney Lake, near Peterborough, Ontario. From entering the immigration office, to being hired and settling in a very pleasant cottage, took just three days. In the years to come I often thought of this immigration officer. He allowed us to make such an auspicious start in our new country.

Those who have experienced Ontario cottage country in the summer do not forget the deep blue sky, the many green islands and the waterways with the soft warm water. I had the better part of enjoying this beautiful landscape outdoors whereas Gusti did the cooking inside, sometimes for up to 16 people instead of only the 4 family members during the week. She simplified cooking by starting to make use of more canned foods which I ferried from McCracken Landing.

Cottage guests of Mr. Webb, who was head of Cofield Brown and Company, usually stayed a week because in 1951 it took about 4½ hours to get there from Toronto. Most of the guests were businessmen such as the then Mayor of Toronto and the Vice President of British Oil Co., or other advertising executives. Some of them wanted to give Gusti tips of five dollar bills when they left. After some hesitation, she took them. I remember trying to avoid responding to questions by guests as much as possible so as to avoid Mr. Webb's annoyance.

We did not spend any money during the two months except for some cigarettes which I was still smoking at the time. We were able to pay for the $200.00 tuition fee by the fall. Mr. & Mrs. Webb suggested that we move into their Toronto home. Gusti could do the cooking and I could study. But she declined saying she would rather do something closer to what she had done in the business field. I had some experience in doing personal service. You might have substantial benefits and interact with people of substance, but you are still a subordinate.

So the die was cast. By Labour Day weekend we were back in Toronto. What a change! It was a beautiful fall day but now the grasses were mostly brown and the pavement hot. We managed to settle Gusti's effects into the basement of No. 12 McGill Street including her prized horsehair mattresses which, being German, were the wrong size for Canadian bed frames. Our attic flat consisted of a single room with some open shelves, one closet, one chair, one twin bed and a table with a small electric hot plate on it. We were certainly crammed in there but happy to be on our own. We shared a bathroom with two other tenants. The first order of business was to thoroughly and repeatedly clean this. We were then ready to go job hunting and to explore the university and its graduate school of business. Almost immediately Gusti found a job as an assistant junior accountant at $32.50 a week. I was accepted for the second year of postgraduate studies at the School of Business Administration, University of Toronto. There were about 20 Canadians and 1 German, me, taking the course.

We still had an emergency fund of a few dollars and the budget improved by two weekly raises of $2.50 each. During Christmas time I delivered mail at the downtown post office starting at 5:00 a.m., three times daily. Fifty years later and considering all factors properly, today's post office comes in second best. It is possible that this semi-government institution simply by definition cannot work well. All I observed then was that the posties really moved the mail. Around this time we thought it would be a good idea to get used to ironed shirts, especially in preparation for upcoming job interviews at the School of Graduate Studies. We had the cash to buy a small iron but wanted to establish our credit rating. So we walked over to Eaton's Yonge and College Street store and asked for credit but were turned down because of insufficient earnings. A decidedly unfriendly clerk suggested that I work first before asking for credit. As a result, for many years, we shopped very little at Eaton's. It did very well for itself over the years without us, but in the end we did better; they went bankrupt.

I remember only some details during the last part of 1951. There was the Hart House Cafeteria at lunchtime where I had a small chocolate milk with my daily peanut butter sandwiches. I looked at the physical education area but did not have the time to make use of it. Studying was mostly done in the reading room at Hart House, our attic room being too small, and at night, too warm. There was very little socializing or of asking a friend over. There simply was not enough room to sit down. Some time after New Year's, company representatives came to the school to evaluate master degree candidates and to offer them employment. Some were interviewed several times. It was the American lieutenant from Boston at the Countess Bucher Estate near Starnberg who helped me to improve my speaking of English, leaving me with a very slight Bostonian accent. It was thanks to him that I could do reasonably well, going into interviews with some assurance.

Before meeting with senior management personnel for the first time, I looked for companies which I would not really like to work for. If one offered me a job I could decline but would have gained valuable interview experience. This is what happened in the case of Canada Packers Ltd. but not in the case of Shell Oil Ltd. I was interviewed with another fellow Canadian candidate, then asked to come to the Toronto head office for a more detailed evaluation. I was then told the decision was made to offer the job to the other candidate. It was pointed out that we both had very impressive backgrounds and were highly qualified. However, I might encounter employee resentment and cause difficulties on account of the very recent war. Leaving the Shell Oil building, I was of course disappointed but not resentful. I thanked them for the chance to be considered and I really meant it. After all, I came to this country for a job but could not expect to find one at any time. Other opportunities would arise and indeed one did, for the Ford Company in Windsor. After I was interviewed and received a job offer, I decided I wanted to stay in Toronto.

I was interested in working for Wood Gundy Ltd. and asked for an interview but did not get one. The company that I was truly interested in was International Business Machines but they did not come to the school for interviews, so I went on my own initiative. At the Toronto regional head office at King and Yonge, a receptionist made several phone calls and then a secretary took me to the manager for me to make my request in detail. I wanted to become an IBM sales representative for large business machines involving punch card accounting systems. They were exceptionally well paid. I felt I could qualify. I had made sure to read up on the company's products, sales and its history. This was an impressive organization and so was the manager I was looking at, tall, impeccably dressed in a somber dark suit and white shirt, as most IBM men were. He listened to my request to work for IBM, then started to look into my background. For the first time in my life I was close to a business executive of substance. I observed his somewhat austere presence and managed to conduct myself with some confidence and assurance. I was told to come and see him again.

At the second interview he asked more detailed questions such as the following. "Let us assume you are now calling on an important customer. He notices your German accent and finds out that you only very recently arrived from Germany. Let us also assume that the customer is Jewish and resentful of your nationality. How would you handle this?" My response was as follows: "I would say that I am sorry to hear about all your people who died or suffered. I mourn my people and remember them as well. I had no responsibility for or knowledge of what happened in the recent sordid past." The Manager and others in the company must have felt that I would not be a deterrent to some customers. He accepted what I presented to him but said I would have to meet and as well convince the IBM National Sales Manager in Don Mills, Ontario. This would take weeks, and would be too close to final exams. I had to secure a job right away. I did get an interview with the Burrows Company Ltd. for closely related large accounting machines in Toronto. I got an interview, received an offer, signed it and started to work for this company in July, 1952.

When the last seminar took place everybody congratulated each other and decided to go for a special lunch. We ended up celebrating until late. Gusti usually made supper for us at our attic apartment. When I came home and opened the door I saw a carefully prepared meal sitting on the small table beside our electric hot plate. A candle had gone out, the food was cold and the tears had dried. I had truly disappointed her. Even after many years, a memory returns evoking strong feelings of regret.

1920 Grandmother Omi

1921 Mother Lilly Bruns

1928 Skiing in Arosa with Madi and my bobsledding friend

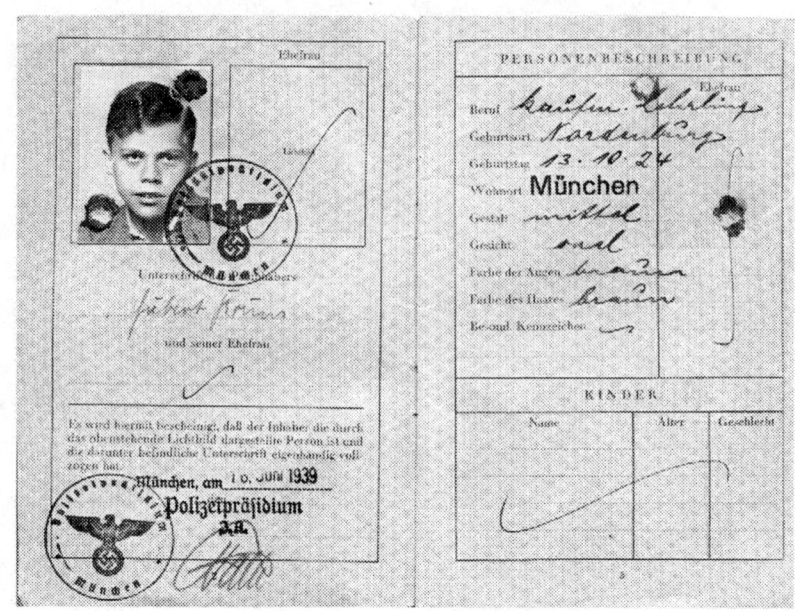

1939 Passport without parent

1944 Motorcycle messenger during air raids

10

UPS AND DOWNS

We began to settle in. Gusti got several raises; I attended training sessions and went out to observe senior salesmen at large accounting installations. We bought a car and went skiing at Mont Tremblant over Christmas, 1952/53 and did a bit of socializing. It is surprising how things changed in a few months. I was still learning about accounting systems but occasionally was told to pick up a small manual adding machine, go downtown door-to-door demonstrating and selling it. I was successful and as a result the company proposed to raise my starting salary and make me the Ontario representative for small adding machines to be sold by independent retailers and promoted by me. I was assured that at any time I could go back and continue training for accounting systems for much higher earnings.

So I found myself calling on customers about twice weekly throughout Southern Ontario. I learned a lot about people there but found this type of travelling exhausting after awhile. About this time our son, Walter, was born, September 11, 1953. We had been apartment sitting for a friend. Now, we had to move into a small apartment. New demands had to be faced and met mostly by Gusti. She carried the little family. I had not looked enthusiastically forward to having, and looking after, a baby. When the time came I felt inept and unsure of myself. It took quite some time to adequately relate to this new being called Walter.

A child, a new, very small apartment, an office job for Gusti, and me constantly travelling started to wear on the family. I was still paid a small salary rather than commission earnings. Instead of waiting for a raise, I convinced myself I should be on my own and make real money. I found out I could sell effectively and had contacts to take over some exclusive items and develop others. I resigned but after a few years discovered that most of them did not prove to become consistent sellers. I had taken quite a chance, lost and had to get back into a job. For the first time I failed with something that was important to me.

An extensive psychological assessment was made for me at the time, which was very laudable and helped in getting into the stationery company Warwick Bros. & Rutter Ltd. When I received the report Gusti very attentively read it and made the comment: "If you are that good how come you are not rich?" To this very day I have not really understood this comment or my feelings at the time. Perhaps she used to be impressed by me, but now lost her belief in me. I began to do some doubting about why I succeed and impress myself. Was it quite a bit of luck or had it been that more intrinsic excellence was at work here? At any rate, I noticed a change in Gusti's demeanor and the occasional look indicating that she saw in me a somewhat less than impressive persona.

I did find a good job largely because of the psychological report. I was appointed sales manager for Warwick, an old established stationery company which had fallen behind the times. I was to revitalize it by introducing new and improved items and to help reverse the company's fortune. I went into this challenge with enthusiasm, hard work and all the ability I could muster. Some items and lines became quite successful but overall the company could not be turned around and eventually had to go into bankruptcy. I had to share in what happened. I spent too much time with the president instead of selling. Each of us needed to have done better.

Until the bankruptcy I was paid well. Our little family kept on skiing in the winter and camping in the summer. We had a Porsche and a sailboat at the Toronto shoreline. Walter had started in kindergarten after speaking mostly German at home. On the face of it everything seemed to move well. Then the increasingly desperate effort to produce profits bore down on me. I worked incessantly, disregarding family considerations most of the time. There were signs of depression. I read Time magazine obsessively at home instead of attending to what had to be done. A lawyer acquaintance was also reading who-done-its in his office very late at night. We both were trying to get out from under respective psychological problems.

In spite of doing well financially Gusti and I started to have serious doubts about each other. We had been a good team but not used to opening up and sharing concerns. Gusti always was an excellent mother, but both of us should have been more companionable and outgoing. She used to be delighted in whatever success I had. Now that there was little of it, she would remonstrate with me. Perhaps she had to take back the emotions which she had been investing in me. I began to talk to Walter and only indirectly to Gusti. The business and then the personal relationship became hopeless and she left with Walter, moving into a new apartment in 1961. I stayed in mine. A good marriage had changed slowly and ended abruptly.

Of all the emotions experienced before and after the break-up, there was one which will always stay sharply etched in my mind. Walter was in Grade Three at Brock Public School then. I came along the fence and found him there, at recess. He saw me and came over; both of us were in tears. A line in Exodus came to me, something about inimitability and the sins of the father being visited upon the son. In whatever ways, I feared I had cast a permanent shadow upon Walter's psyche. I very much hope it has now receded into his unconscious.

Suddenly, I found myself being on my own. Sometimes I was stunned with a slight headache. At those moments I would regret what happened, especially in regard to Walter. However, I did not stay at loose ends. Right away I started to do daily exercises, got a new apartment and furnished it, looked for a job and found one as a sales manager for Canadian Charts Ltd. in Oakville, Ontario. I was on my own once more. Approximately every second weekend I had Walter with me. At first, we were not very much at ease with each other in spite of my effort to be myself. This was brought home to me, visually and audibly, in a Swiss Chalet Restaurant of all places. With Walter sitting beside me, I observed what was obviously a father and his young son being noticeably ill at ease with each other but trying their best not to be. I thought of this father and others hoping to find solace. As time went on Walter reverted to his natural and open self.

I did well enough in my new job in Oakville but I was not working the way I used to. I had put everything into my last job, all I was capable of, with enthusiasm, determination and enormous effort. I had two considerable business failures on my record in a string of noticeable accomplishments. The former showed a tendency to disregard long-term objectives. In short, it could be said that I was not as good as I thought I was.

I did not think in those terms; I was more concerned about Walter and not taking another massive assignment. Preferably I would like to spend more time with him and less with accomplishing goals.

Teaching seemed a possibility. I had two academic degrees. All I needed was to obtain the necessary teaching certification. I checked with the College of Education in London, Ontario, went through its curriculum and was accepted. I resigned my job in Oakville, sub-let my apartment in Toronto and moved to London. I studied for the required one year, became a specialist high school teacher and started with the Etobicoke Board of Education in 1965.

At 42 years of age, in 1965 I found myself in a brand new Ontario high school, West Humber Collegiate Institute, with over 1200 students and 110 teachers in Grades 9 to 13. I taught four different subjects per day to 25 students mostly in Grade 11 to 13 (later 12). I could call on quite a bit of experience teaching high school Economics, Grade 12 Law and Sociology and Grade 11 Business Mathematics and Computer Programming.

In 1967 the Etobicoke Board of Education and West Humber Collegiate for the first time installed an IBM computer the size of a large desk with two punch-card units. I learned to operate this computer using the Fortran language in order to write a course outline for teaching high school students in programming. While I was occupied writing this course and teaching at the same time I found out that for some time small desk-top personal computers were emerging. An entirely new and exciting industry arose. Being part of it would mean that I would face a major challenge to my ability and be again very much involved beyond my present career. I decided against another new venture. Instead I wanted to be more with Walter as both of us went to school and beyond.

Teaching high school turned out to be quite an experience. I had never been in one until I taught. My schooling consisted of public school Grades 1 to 4 in Switzerland, 5 to 8 in Germany with a self-taught part of some Grade 13 subjects. All other schooling produced two university degrees. My students were astonished that I never studied in high school. I in turn realized quickly that I needed to learn more about adolescent group behaviour. Students stayed particularly docile for weeks and allowed a teacher to be blissfully unaware of resentment. All of a sudden the tiger is revealed and let loose. Proper discipline and acceptable teaching is gone with nothing but constant damage control or complete failure.

From the first day of school the teacher has to set a standard and keep it. This is most important in the first weeks and months up to Christmas. He must constantly aim at all students. Presentation, eye contact, demeanor and voice must be evenly maintained. He should focus on his subject, not the students or himself. This is difficult to achieve but I adopted a successful method. As in a lion's cage in the circus, the trainer does not really threaten the animals. Rather he maintains absolute control through eye and body movement. Magnetism seems to be at work here for the trainer and the animals. At times they actually move to pounce but think better of it. The trainer's excellent performance keeps him in charge and alive. A teacher will do well in a classroom provided he has established behaviour conducive to learning. Some otherwise quite assertive personalities cannot do that.

1951 Scholarship Exchange Student

1970 Teacher in Toronto

1987 Jackson Hole   Wyoming

1996 With my wife Janet and my sister Madi

11

MY SON WALTER

By the time I had started to teach, Walter and I had already been to Munich to see his Grandmother. He spoke fluent German at home and at all times when possible. We continued to ski together through the years to come and we always had a good time with each other. For example, one week we skied at Jay Peaks in Vermont until Sunday afternoon. Then we had to get home to Toronto, past Montreal, in my Volkswagen. It got dark and started to snow. Both of us were desperately trying to stay awake but found it increasingly difficult to do so. It occurred to us not just to talk but to think of and to move our minds to specific images and discuss them so as to stay awake. So I asked Walter to explain to me in detail how the planet Earth rotates and moves around the sun. In return and in between I explained the concept of inflation and deflation, and some other economic thoughts. In the middle of a question, Walter could not last any longer. He nodded and his head fell forward; he was completely out. I turned off my lane as far as I could, put a blanket over him, fell asleep and woke up very cold some time later. He came to when we arrived in Toronto.

The two of us were together on most weekends, and of course on most long school holidays, making the best use of our time, and of each other. There was skiing at Collingwood near Toronto and there were out-of-country ski trips to the Hafelecar in Innsbruck, Austria, Zermat in Switzerland, the

Zugspitze in Germany, Snowbird and Alta in Utah and to Jackson Hole in Wyoming. There were several summer holidays to Germany and the most memorable, a five-week first-class Eurail trip to ten different countries in Europe.

Walter was fifteen years old at the time and an absolute delight to travel with. I got hold of a very realistic toy hand gun of the type not yet restricted. My sister Madi made a shoulder holster for him to carry it and protect us on the journey. He would observe the platform goings-on and at the last minute board the train. At times I could see him through a window but sometimes he would be at the other end. I was quite certain he would not get left behind but after the train was on its way again I admit I did keep glancing in the aisle for him to appear. He always did. Through several years of experience I found that he was very reliable and would not take unreasonable chances. This is pretty well all that can be expected from an intelligent youngster.

The grand European trip of 1968 started in our home town of Munich, proceeded to Wiesbaden to see my Grandparents' old place, then continued down the Rhine by boat to Cologne. A boy about Walter's age described the castles on either side with a perfect Frankfurt-area dialect that I found difficult to follow but which Walter had no trouble with. Then and on other later occasions I realized how easily he could imitate languages and learn to speak them. We always took city buses to go sight-seeing and to visit attractions but could not see or appreciate all that was to be seen. From touring the cathedral and Cologne we went to Hamburg and took a ferry ride to see its extensive harbour installation, then to Copenhagen where unfortunately Walter had an asthma attack. We arrived late at the hotel and immediately went to sleep. Next morning I waited for Walter in the lobby glancing

1953 This new being called Walter

1968 Shades of James Bond
Walter protecting his Dad

1972 Physics student at U. of T.

Walter and Tracy Bruns 1995

at brochures. To my considerable surprise I found several very explicit illustrated porno books which at that time were not displayed in Germany. I hung around until Walter came down. I wanted his reaction and I got it. He thought we should buy them and he would sell them to his friends!

Since the weather was not pleasant we decided to move to Paris. There was more than enough to see there and we strolled through the avenues or sat down trying to pick up the ambiance of this place. The next long train ride got us from Paris south to Lisbon in Portugal and then to a small seaside resort to recuperate. Much as I tried only Walter properly pronounced "obrigado" (thank you). For the next trip he sat up front with the engineer of the electric engine looking at the unfolding Spanish landscape to Madrid, something I never did. At that time, I rarely looked at masters' paintings or reflected on them but Goya's 'Third of May 1808' at the Prado in Madrid stayed powerfully in our minds.

The night train took us to Barcelona and a few days later to Marseille and the Cote d'Azur. Eighteen years ago I had come here from Munich on the way to America. I remarked about it and a quite elderly lady in our first-class compartment spoke up with a few words in German. Walter took over in French and the two conversed nicely. I remember it because of her two extraordinarily beautiful diamond rings.

Before the beginning of the trip I wondered about how to stay within our budget and not have Walter ask for extras if possible. I hit upon what I thought was a good idea and suggested I would hand over to him all the cash for the trip and he would pay for everything. This worked very well indeed except when for example I wanted to have another coffee and he decided we could do without it. He always got the check, first made corrections if needed, did the addition, checked that and paid for it. He decided on lodgings and negotiated if necessary. More often than not I stayed in the background because he would do better, so there was never any disagreement. He was a first-rate tour guide. In Rome, I was laid up by a kidney colic. I felt out of sorts but tried to see the sights as much as possible anyway. I was always fascinated by jewelry so we went in to see beautiful displays, especially diamonds. I also wanted to look at cuff links because I always fancied a pair. I picked up a heavy set with an excellent design in 18 carat gold but it was far too expensive and I felt I could not afford it. Walter's mother had given him a bit of cash to buy some souvenirs. He decided on an expensive heavy gold charm for a bracelet for her. I paid for it with some hesitation being envious of Walter's degree of affection and also at the same time feeling cheap.

It was very hot in Rome and we decided not to continue to Naples. Instead we turned north to the Alps through what used to be Austria's south Tyrol. We saw Innsbruck again looking at the Havelecar Mountains where we had skied a year ago in the winter. There I became ill with pneumonia and Walter had to lead me home all the way to Toronto and into my apartment. A fabulous time was had by the two of us, with lots of memories to be stored. As the years go by some of them may unexpectedly come up and into focus, recalling a delightful happening. I will never forget these memories with Walter; may they stay with him and overcome others of the past.

Occasionally I complained about kidney pain and stayed overnight in hospital for some small stones to pass. Other than the occasional ailments I was in good condition even though I had started to smoke when I was about 16. As I got older I smoked more, as so many others did. I never had any trouble with coughing or doing exercises. I liked smoking especially while reading or writing. By now I had advanced to smoking up to 40 cigarettes a day. One particular morning, I woke up and reached for the first one of the day, along with my lighter and special filter holder. I am not sure why I hesitated to light up. Perhaps something in my subconscious felt I was overdoing things, what with 40 cigarettes a day and even more later on. So why not think about quitting altogether? Indeed why not?

This of course was easy to say and to promise but how could such a promise be kept? I had been able to make promises to myself and keep them but would I be able to do so again in this case? To begin with it would be a good idea for me to promise not to smoke for one day. It could not possibly be that difficult. Surely I could hang in there. I made it and was pleased with myself. I now continued not to smoke and decided to promise not to smoke under any circumstances for one complete week. Just to be on the safe side, I stipulated that if it became unbearable I would never the less do my very utmost to wait until the week-end for blessed relief. It seemed that this would be a fail-proof solution.

Not smoking for a week was increasingly difficult to manage. To satisfy my constant cravings I started to chew mints, which only added a desire to eat more. But I resisted! I wanted to stay in shape but now I had another constant urge to contend with adding misery to my trouble. I tried to feel satisfaction in not having smoked, having done it without help. Increasingly, will power started to outweigh the power of the addiction within me. Obviously I was not yet really through with it. But I made progress and felt I could prevail. With the courage of my convictions I decided not to smoke for another full month.

The next month started off with even more of a desire to smoke again. I wanted and needed it as much as I ever wanted anything. I was beside myself and could work only intermittently. At times I was overwhelmed and in those moments I came close to defeat. I had made up my mind to have an open pack of cigarettes and my lighter with me at all times. I would offer one to a smoker saying he should have one but that I did not need one. I realized that this was not very nice but I needed every bit of self-esteem I could muster. I was constantly aware of an overpowering force within me that was almost stronger than I was. Even the excruciating kidney pains I had experienced were not so insidious. Utter despair overwhelmed me at times. I had never prayed before or asked for such an intervention. In my mind images appeared together with parts of sermons from my youth in church. I asked what I had done, why had I been forsaken and not allowed to be released. At times I came close to tears.

There was nothing I could do except bear the suffering. Then gradually the force of my addiction subsided and my need to smoke abated. I had gone through the worst and thought of the words from the Bible: "He restoreth my soul, he leadeth me in the paths of righteousness for his name's sake." As the storm lessened I was again determined to prevail and continued an additional non-smoking vigil for another three months. Then the hour arrived and the monkey was off my back for good. A tremendous effort had been made to keep resisting. Subconsciously I was traumatized as evidenced three years later when I woke up in a sweat and absolute panic. I dreamed vividly that I had smoked but then realized I had not and would not ever again.

I felt released, ready to take on something new. I always liked and appreciated girls and they in turn seemed to be reasonably interested in me. When I was about fifteen and curious to know about them I asked my mother if I was good looking. She laughed, smiled and said, "Yes, as long as you show affection and enthusiasm." There must have been something like that when I met a young medical doctor whom I called Pooh the Bear. We corresponded by letter, then later met in Prague. I got her to come to Vienna, then brought her to Toronto. It was a difficult decision but I felt that I should not get married after all. Basically she was inclined to be too much of a hippy. I had less of such leanings and was really a conservative. This could also be explained differently by saying that I was a bit scared.

I have been fortunate in meeting interesting females. I admit as I got older they got younger. It was not a matter of preference but simply of happenchance and association with for example friends skiing with Walter. I felt privileged to meet and associate with a number of companions but did not really think of another marriage. I might have come close but kept in mind my age as well as theirs; I was now over fifty. Then I met the chance of a lifetime. After four years of a very close and very beautiful relationship, my companion, nicknamed "Muli", said she would marry me in spite of the difference in our ages. One day she stood in front of a full-length bathroom mirror adjusting her hair and smiling at me as I stood at her side with my chin leaning on her shoulder, both faces close together. There she was, the embodiment of youth and beauty and there was I, the image of on-setting old age. There was a moment of truth. She could face it but I could not. Later, she asked me to come to her wedding and I did, sitting at the back. Thirty years have gone by now; I am still here with my memories.

In the sixties, a lot of German immigrants came to Toronto, followed by Italians. Italians usually came in family units making small payments on low-priced homes. All family members would immediately get to work on renovations, start to reduce the mortgage and increase the equity. Germans usually came as singles and located in rooming houses in the core of the city. Some made down payments on higher priced houses, renting every possible space to others. Often immigrants needed to speak better English. However, skilled workers were in demand. I remember going to a service station with a friend who needed a job but could not speak any English. He got the job within the hour. At that time, statistically speaking every fourth person in Toronto was a German.

A fellow German I met had difficulty writing his University of Toronto B.A. thesis on the assimilation of a group of German ethnics. I undertook to help him and suggested he should gather the relevant written material and read it. He would explain and discuss it in detail with me. I would then develop the methodology and dictate the thesis to him. In effect, I could say that I wrote and produced his thesis. It should be noted however that in my opinion the sociology in this thesis contained a lot of repetition and wordy pronouncements that were merely common sense. He received his degree. We continued to co-operate by finding medium-sized rural real estate properties, mostly farms that could be subject to subdivision. He would find one and subdivide; I would sell the parcels on a commission basis without a license. This of course entailed spending a lot of time on weekends and school breaks. I advertised in the Toronto papers, got some response, phoned back, outlined property and location, and arranged to meet clients there. Hopefully, they came. If not I returned home tired and disappointed. Eventually some homes in Toronto were also bought and sold. I continued teaching until 1982 and participated in more real estate ventures until 1988 when I retired. Riches had not come my way but I did well and would rather be with Walter at ease, in good health and with friends.

Walter continued to do excellent work in school throughout public and high school. He continued to show evidence of a first-rate mind. When he was about eight years old, a mechanical engineer came to the apartment to show me a sketch of his new printing press that could automatically produce calendars. Walter was asked to remain in the bedroom, not to interrupt, and to stay with his small but accurate drafting board. About two hours later the engineer left and Walter came into the living room with some sketches of the printing press and gave them to me. I looked at them very closely in detail, found them as projected and essentially complete. How he could draw like this and come up with such a highly technical design, on the basis of just listening next door, was and still is beyond me.

Up to the time he earned his M.A. Degree in Physics in 1978, Walter and I were together quite often. His mother had remarried but Walter did not spend much time with his stepfather; yet Walter was not unappreciative of him and neither was I. Aside from winter skiing and summer trips, we played tennis and chess with time to exchange thoughts, ideas and opinions. I had learned mostly through indiscriminate reading; there had been little systematic schooling. I was left to emulate logical constructs on my own, doing my best against Walter's increasing competence in matters of thinking and expression. I must have overdone this in a particular instance resulting in the following exchange. He felt he should perhaps stay away from me. I asked why and added I surely had the best answer to his question. The reply came that this was precisely why he should stay away from me. It was said in humour but also with some emphasis behind it.

There had always been humour between us, being alike in many ways with an assurance of similar beliefs. Some anxieties may have been present on occasion in both of us but they did not show much. I remember the time when Walter had been truly concerned about marriage. We had been on holidays in the Caribbean and I found him very distraught but he did not go further or come closer. On another occasion it was I who really wanted to share my dismay. In the hospital a kidney stone was operated on and less than a week later the entire kidney had to be removed. The mere thought of being cut up again in the exact same place with an additional hernia and disfigurement drove me into a severe depression. The hospital psychiatrist did not help me much. One has to learn how to cope by oneself.

If at all possible one should also learn to place some especially disagreeable memories into a special compartment and store them there securely. You can then open this compartment and peruse what is in there, to review its content and if needed learn and perhaps correct mistakes. The content can then be put back into its special compartment leaving all other memories free to roam at will. Things hastily swept under the carpet are bound to keep popping up especially in dreams unless some sort of psychic order is established. It is difficult by oneself to sort out and identify conflicting emotions. Close relatives may not be able to help much.

At the close of the seventies I had again gone to visit my mother. She was up and about, able to go for meals, although only slowly on my arm to the large dining room. As I went in I was struck by the number of old people that were assembled there. For a moment I felt she was not really one of them. She was talking as she always did with assurance and without being aware of the obvious sounds and movements of old age. On the way back up to her room she paused and looked at me saying, "Let us say good-bye to each other now. We may not see or talk again." A short time later I went again to see her in Munich but she was in bed and without awareness or recognition. She had said good-bye in her inimitable way. She died in 1981 at 89 years of age. Life should have done much better by her but she never pleaded in protest. She had compassion, humour, ability and above all a strong will which I hope to emulate. I stand in awe of her and always will. Would that the heavens above still hear what I always felt about her; she would be happy.

12

NEW BEGINNINGS

I already mentioned that I had not married again. Then after twenty odd years having interesting female friends I found one of the long-lasting type to be with. I got together with Janet Sankey who taught instrumental music and English at West Humber Collegiate. She also played violin, viola and piano. We explored the possibility of staying together. This became love and still is. In 1979, I had renovated a four-plex apartment building at 62 Gothic Avenue. We decided in 1981 to live there in two separate apartments. There were summer holidays and winter ski trips, some with Janet's daughter, Tanah. I liked being taken by Janet to symphony concerts, catching up with culture.

There were happy times with the High Park Ski Club, ski trips to Vermont and Quebec and staying at Gray Rocks, where Janet learned to ski well. In the summer we windsurfed and Janet became good at that too. I took her to Munich to meet my family. In 1979 my mother suggested saying good-bye to each other not knowing when we might meet again. In 1980 she did not know me any more. So Janet met my mother only through photos yet she feels about my mother the way I do. My mother would have approved of Janet whole-heartedly. Here is just one indication. In 1986, standing in the Seeshaupt Square on a beautiful summer morning with my sister, a Remembrance Day band struck up a very moving German soldiers' lament as the names of the fallen were called out one by one. Tears were in many eyes including Janet's.

For our 1985 summer vacation we decided to see the west coast of British Columbia and Vancouver Island. I had never been out west, always going to Europe to visit with relatives. Janet's sister lived near Trail and let us use her somewhat aged Westfalia camper. We drove off to Banff to visit Walter who had started his career with Canadian Mountain Holidays. No wonder he wanted to stay in this part of the province. Driving west to Vancouver, over to Victoria and exploring the Island, we were awestruck by what we saw. Sometimes we would see an exceptionally nice view and imagine we would locate and build a home for ourselves there. The dreams receded as we headed east going home but we knew we would return.

We had fallen in love with the Westfalia camper and forthwith did something about it. One was ordered and paid for with delivery to take place in the Spring of 1986 at the factory in Northern Germany. In the meantime we assembled all necessary camping equipment, pots, pans, sleeping bags and clothing, into two large duffle bags to be taken later on the plane. In the spring I flew to Frankfurt and went by train to the factory with the two heavy bags and my other luggage. I had a day to familiarize myself with the camper and to store everything, then drove to the Frankfurt airport and picked up Janet. We started on our six-week European camping trip with absolutely everything prepared including some food. It turned out that after all there was only one item missing. A funnel was wanted and described in Italy but we were unable to find an 'imbuto'.

With our Westfalia camper, we lived in comfort, cooking, eating, sleeping, sight-seeing and driving through eight countries in six weeks. There were many special highlights to remember. My cousin, Lore took us to the magnificent Gothic cathedral in Ulm. Janet climbed its tower showing no fear of heights but I declined. As already mentioned, my sister Madi took us to a very moving Remembrance Day ceremony in Seeshaupt. Then there were many hairpin turns driving up to Arosa, Switzerland, my childhood home. Driving in Italy required nerves of steel and fast reflexes. We were not used to horns blaring and drivers cursing each other. "Bastardo!" was a common shout. We parked the camper near train stations in the big cities of Milan, Florence and Rome and took tour buses to see the sights. In many art galleries and museums, graduate students were excellent guides.

In Greece, after visiting Delphi Janet suffered from heat exhaustion. I found a lovely shade tree near a cistern and put her feet in the cool water—no oracle. After Athens and antiquity we had a beautiful night sleeping on the top deck of the ferry to Crete, looking up at millions of stars in the clear sky. The camper was perfect for sight-seeing all over Crete. We went north through Thermopylae, Macedonia and Yugoslavia, through Austria and back to Germany. A most memorable time was had in our trusted VW camper.

Janet flew back to Toronto. I drove to Emden and shipped the Westfalia to Albany, New York, all camping equipment and roof rack included. I went back to Frankfurt and flew to Toronto. Six weeks later I went to Albany to pick up the Westfalia and drove it through the U.S. border at Lewiston into Canada and to Toronto. I was tired but pleased that everything had gone well when all of a sudden I realized that nothing whatsoever had been mentioned or declared by me at the Canadian Customs. Sooner, rather than later, I decided to go back through both the Canadian as well as the U.S. borders, turn around and go to Canadian Customs to somewhat belatedly pay the appropriate duty on the Westfalia and its license.

Janet, Tanah and I decided in late 1986 to spend two weeks over Christmas in a resort near Cumana, Venezuela. Being allowed to bring my Mistral windsurfer on the plane for free was the clincher. I had to build a wheeled wooden carrier to move the heavy 12-foot windsurfer to and from the airport by myself. This turned out to be quite a chore. Early in the morning of departure thousands of Christmas vacationers were jammed into the Toronto terminal as step-by-step I cajoled and pushed my construction toward the counter, with Janet and Tanah carrying our luggage right behind me. Some vacationers, ticket agents and even a supervisor helped me to move my board and put it over the counter. He then smiled a bit, looked at me and said, "No problem." Later on people on the beach treated me and I let them use my board, which was the best board on the bay. A bus trip into the mountains and jogging on the beach very early in the mornings rounded up this vacation except for the return of Janet's missing luggage three months later.

In 1987 and again in 1988 we drove to British Columbia with our Westfalia and explored the possibility of finding a house or lot to build, preferably somewhere on the lower mainland. By accident we found a lot in Maple Bay close to Duncan and Victoria on Vancouver Island. Walking through the two-acre lot with its spectacular view of the bay we realized that this would be the ideal place. An offer was made in twenty-four hours, countered, offered again and accepted. We had our place in paradise. Now we looked for an architect and contractor but decided to defer decisions for awhile.

13

A CEREBRAL INCIDENT

My official retirement was coming up in October. I would be 65. On September 15, 1988, after eating supper I was not feeling well so I went downstairs to try to feel a bit better and turned on the TV. It showed something about the last 100 days of WWII and Hitler. This was depressing enough the way I was feeling so I turned it off. Janet came down, having finished her schoolwork and noticed the way I must have looked but I insisted I would feel all right shortly. I was obviously not. I got a severe headache and began to throw up. Janet phoned for an ambulance which arrived, but by now I was only partially conscious and absolutely refused to go with the attendants. They would not force me. I crawled into the farthest corner of my bed with a pounding headache and vomited heavily into a pail. The sickness came over me. I felt it was the end.

Janet desperately needed help and again phoned. This time an ambulance came with a doctor. He told her my condition was serious and I should be hospitalized immediately. He spoke to me harshly but I did not respond and moved away from him. He told Janet I could not be removed by force. He told her to check on me every half hour then left with the ambulance. Janet was now alone in the house with me. In the darkness before morning she must have been beside herself and dreadfully worried about what was happening.

I must have come to at times with less vomiting until in the morning my good friend and helper, Joe with Janet managed to get me into my car and took off for St. Joseph's Hospital. I think I had some awareness of being moved and even thought I could dimly see part of the hospital building approaching but remember nothing more from there on in. Self-awareness did not exist any more; the light within me had gone out. Like a dimmer switch it did come back in a few days but just barely as I mouthed Janet's name calling her 'honey'. Some more recognition took place. I was told there had been a cerebral incident. In other words I had had a stroke and was lucky to be alive.

Life began again but it seemed different. I was dazed and disoriented. Then I realized that I could not really talk any more. What I came up with were disjointed words haltingly repeated. Some neurological patients at the hospital could not talk any more at all; others were more or less paralyzed. I was not that badly off and I was determined to talk and think coherently again. Walter came to visit and I complained bitterly about my condition. I felt sorry for myself. He suggested more selective listening instead. For just a moment I was truly taken aback. Then I stopped feeling sorry for myself but not without a somewhat hollow laugh.

First of all, I had to get back into more and better talking. I also had to try and comprehend what happened within my mind. I always felt that the way to become coherent would be to express everything well. My attempt at learning to speak English by myself many years ago was repeated once more in the hospital. I put simple and short sentences together and memorized them, as children learn to speak. They hear distinct sounds and repeat them; in due course letters, words and sentences evolve. Like everybody else I had a tendency to interrupt but now I discovered that I was cutting myself off, so to speak. In the middle of a sentence the words would disappear, much like a short circuit disconnects, leaving me to try and recall from memory or to search about for a substitute word. At other times, the first word would suddenly come back. It might be possible to re-establish connections in the mind but that would take time. In the meantime, I was frustrated and left in mid-air.

I concentrated on ways of improving my mind. I have always been fascinated by how really involved sentences come into being. In grammar, you construct a sentence. Logic determines correct thinking. I used to be able to dictate fluently even difficult material. I was good at constructing sentences adding perhaps an occasional touch of eloquence. Now I was reduced to simple sentences, more often than not haltingly produced. I did my best to think more purposefully and not just gaze out through the window. Janet was still teaching but came to see me every evening and weekends. Some friends visited and a very supportive speech therapist worked with me.

I left the hospital feeling that I had changed but the change was difficult to put into precise terms. I thought I was more within myself, more introspective because of the intense mental contemplation I had tried to do. At the same time I felt lonely but reminded myself that I was indeed lucky to have had only minor mental impairments and no physical handicaps. I recalled some lines in Shakespeare's Richard the Third, mentioning "the winter of my discontent". I looked forward to summer and new beginnings.

Throughout the Fall and Winter of 1988/89 I continued to be concerned with the goings on in my mind. I hoped that my talking might improve, thinking might be more coherent and my emotions managed better. I very much wanted to write good sentences again, perhaps even dictate fluently as before. In short I wanted to come close to what I used to be or at least an approximation thereof. I had always tried my best; now I had to try harder.

Working to improve my speech exhausted me. This led to a wish to do more physical work rather than mental exercises. There always had been more of an urge to do than to think. Stroke or no stroke, now I had a chance to do something. The beautiful lot in Maple Bay, near Duncan on Vancouver Island, British Columbia had been secured and paid for. Now an architect and contractor had to be found with Janet deciding on many designs. A small apartment was rented in Duncan and early every morning I would go to the construction site helping to move material and to clean up at the end of each day. In 1990 as our new home was being built, Janet organized and packed our belongings in Toronto. I stored everything in a 24-foot U-haul truck which I drove 4,500 kilometers partly through the United States to Maple Bay in six days. The endless west passed by hour after hour with little need for thinking but enjoying the scenery and feeling at ease.

Janet with our cat Cornflake, flew from Toronto to Vancouver at the end of June. I picked them up at the airport and we headed via the ferry for our new home in Maple Bay. I continued to enjoy physical work. I built some porches, woodsheds and walkways and designed some projects for use on the ocean waterfront. There I was by myself occasionally looking out over the bay to the hills around it. Arbutus and other trees were hiding neighbourhood homes, sunshine rippled over the water and large boats created white wakes. I was happy and not concerned with the workings of my mind.

Meanwhile, Janet tracked down local sources for organic food, studied the flora and fauna of Maple Bay (so different from Ontario!) and did much landscaping and gardening. The freezer was soon full of seasonal produce. She began to teach violin, viola and piano privately and play viola with a variety of groups.

Janet and I knew we were in paradise and in an ideal climate looking only for short occasional holidays. As Goethe asked, why look for luck in far away places if it is already found right here? We found it when we got together and again in Maple Bay.

14

ADVENTURES

In our Volkswagen camper, Janet and I travelled extensively in North America. On one trip in the summer of 1987, we went up by gondola past the rocky cliffs and ragged peaks of Corbet's Couloir at Jackson Hole, Wyoming. I had been skiing there about twenty years ago with Walter and his university friends. I vividly recall I involuntarily dropped and fell into this well-known couloir. At the time, I could not rest with my miserable performance when I fell so I had skied again and successfully jumped into Corbet's Couloir. It could easily have done me in. Janet wanted to know where exactly I had gone down and could not believe it. Neither did I when I got to the precipice and leaned over the edge on my knees, then very carefully moved back. Close to the outside gondola entrance there stood and still is a very cute small wooden bear as a good luck charm. Janet took a picture of him with me so as to keep me out of harm's way and from Corbet's Couloir once more.

The next bear to be noticed was in Yellowstone National Park as we drove west to our Island. He was close to a paved road, very happily alive and foraging in the meadow paying no attention to the lined-up cars except for one photographer who was getting too close. The bear was smart and moved off. The silly human could easily have been killed by the bear. We found out how truly large this national park is by criss-crossing it for days on end, staying in camping grounds every night, trying to get warm in the chilly mornings. Beautiful mountains, meadows and waterfalls—all of them created images to be retained in memory. A few years later we saw the park again after it was extensively burned. I trust the happy bear stayed healthy.

While Janet visited her sister in Fruitvale, B.C., Walter, Mark Kingsbury, Fred Noble and I had gone to windsurf in the Gorge on the Columbia River near Mt. Hood. The three of them were experienced surfers and went back and forth on this well-known fast and strong-flowing river where powerful barges plied on the far side. I didn't think I should cross it but Walter said I should try. So I did, made it across to the far shore, turned, fell and kept getting up only to fall again until I was completely exhausted. Fred came along, jumped in, undid my mast and sail, put them on my board, secured them, told me to float behind, got up on his board and sailed back to the near shore. As I turned my head I could see one of the barges coming up fast. Now I was back on the shore with my rig, stumbling up over huge rocks, through a wire fence and onto the railroad tracks. As a train approached I found how high the engine was above the rail bed. The engineer waved down at me. I took my board and rig across the tracks and then hitchhiked to the campground. I have gone back to the Gorge since but haven't windsurfed.

Another journey was more visual, an exploration down the west coast. This venture started at Victoria in May 1992, going by ferry to Port Angeles then south through the States of Washington, Oregon and California, following closely the coast down to San Francisco. The No. 1 highway would go way up into the mountains or drop to the ocean close enough to jump out and go wading. Every time I turned left and away from a drop-off Janet would lean noticeably left, the same as when we went up the sharp switchback road to Arosa some years ago. We followed the coastline through redwood forests and giant sequoias to the Golden Gate and San Francisco. There, postcard images showed a sparkling bay, lit-up yellow buildings and a very beautiful city.

From there we drove east and camped near Needles, California, beside the Colorado River and the Arizona border. As usual I had done a lot of driving and wanted to get into the river to do some swimming. I went up along the shore to a likely spot, jumped in and caught right away the fast moving current going past where the camper stood. Janet was preparing supper and happened to look up as I passed by. As she watched she saw me as I turned in a small whirlpool, which sent me right back in the opposite direction and close to the shore. I got out as both of us laughed but it was a little bit too funny. After eating and doing the dishes we sat at the open side door of the camper observing the slowly setting sun. Nearby we could hear a harpsichord and alto recorder being played al fresco. We went closer and saw that the people there had a Yamaha keyboard and boxes of music. Janet ended up at the keyboard playing Telemann and Bach, and dozens of songs from Joan Bias, Bob Dylan and other albums with everyone singing along until late into the night.

Early the next morning we were on our way to the Grand Canyon. As we got closer the landscape remained level and there was no indication of anything unusual to be encountered. Then a sharp drop-off was noticed extending left and right; the awesome canyon came into view. At first glance looking down to the river, it seems almost small as it twists and turns away into the far distance. The eye has to concentrate and realize that the riverbed is thousands of feet below. Steep and narrow trails lead down to the canyon floor and to the unbelievable heat. As before a nice campsite close to the action was found and we explored the rim for days, driving and walking.

Only a few tourists were hiking all the way down and up the canyon and some were riding mules. I noticed an especially appealing mule and wanted to touch her. There in my mind I saw the image of my very own "muli" of many years ago. I had given her this pet name and called her a muli because of the innate beautiful animal she was. After all these years I ask that she be allowed to be a real muli once more, without a heavy burden, so that I can continue with my very fond memories.

The U.S. southwest continued in all its glory as we crossed the Colorado River heading for Zion National Park and the Bryce Canyon of red mud. After that we turned north and headed home through Nevada and California's Yosemite National Park sharing crowded campsites, hiking and climbing the Lembert Dome without seeing anybody else around because nearly everybody stayed in the valley. On the way dogwoods were in bloom, giant sequoias were seen and beautiful Lake Tahoe admired. We kept driving north on the Interstate Highway looking left and right at endless fields of vegetables, orchards and vineyards. I was driving and moving as if in suspended animation, yet aware of what was unfolding outside as well as inside of me. The engine at the rear of the camper made practically no noise; there was only the wind rushing by. Janet slept in the rear and I, being by myself, thought of all we had seen. It was almost too much for me. On the other hand I could absorb and remember and felt that I should continue.

That summer we visited Walter in Banff, Alberta. Ever since graduation in 1977 he had moved there to work for Hans

Gmoser and Canadian Mountain Holidays, which had started in 1965. Walter was hooked on the new sport of helicopter skiing and wanted to keep on doing it. I had originally been very concerned because at first this was only short winter employment. I pointed out to him that in line with his academic accomplishments a more suitable occupation should be pursued. In turn he pointed out and wanted to know why he should work in an office for eleven months only to ski for one month. He assured me that when necessary he would be quite capable of finding and keeping suitable employment at any time. I made an attempt to prevail upon him but as it turned out things worked out very well for him. He said he was not in the habit of failing.

Hans Gmoser offered him a job, to begin with driving a bus moving heli skiers in and out of newly built lodges in the remote interior of British Columbia. This was of course winter employment only. Walter used all his time and spare money to systematically work toward professional standing in ski instruction, heli ski guiding, summer and winter mountaineering and related courses, culminating in becoming a certified Canadian and Swiss mountain guide. Founder Hans Gmoser went on to become a legend in his own right and Walter found his idol, vocation and success.

At first Walter designed, renovated and built some smaller CMH additions such as the Bugaboo Bath House, then started to work with the Calgary architect on some new lodges and additions. I can remember the time when he was eight years old and showed me the amazingly accurate sketch of a printing press. He did this listening through a closed door while somebody explained the design to me. Then and now I have no adequate explanation. From his start at Canadian Mountain Holidays in 1977 he progressed to heli guiding in

1986, lodge manager in 1989, chief operating officer in 1991 and president in 2001. When I look at his many accomplishments, I think of him as my pride and joy.

Walter invited Janet and me to spend a week in the latest CMH Adamant Lodge, near Revelstoke, British Columbia, for some heli-hiking. I had been in a helicopter while skiing at CMH but Janet for the first time experienced the excitement of moving effortlessly close to mountain peaks and looking down into steep valleys. Every so often the helicopter would set down on a high plateau to let guests amble about in the meadows or hike out further. At the end of the day we were taken home to the isolated lodge.

We found more than a first-class hotel amidst high mountains. There were large diesel generators, a deep well, a state-of-the-art sewage system and two helicopters that stayed on pads. Inside you notice first-rate furnishings and equipment and meet the highly competent staff. There is complete ease around you. Outside you raise your eyes to the mountains above. They mirror a beautifully designed lodge. The architect Robert Leblond created additional ones. Each inspired design reflects on nature. No doubt Frank Lloyd Wright would approve. At night, standing outside, there is absolute stillness; just a touch of wind may move and whisper in the trees. You are truly alone in the mountains.

In 1995 four years after being appointed an executive at CMH Walter married Tracy Allen. A most spectacular wedding took place close to the top of the Lake Louise ski resort with guests transported up in gondolas. Two lines of CMH ski guides raised their ski poles and made an arch for the newlyweds to be saluted. Hundreds of friends attended the reception at Chateau Lake Louise.

For years now I avoided talking for longer than a few sentences. Instead I tried to listen as Walter had suggested and take in what was presented to me through travelling. In 1995 Janet and I took the camper eastward to Toronto checking on our building there, and travelling on to Ottawa, Montreal and into Pennsylvania to visit relatives. Then we followed Interstate 70 into Saint Louis and its enormous arch commemorating the opening of the Midwest and the mountains of the west. I wanted to go to a small place called Independence, Missouri, to see the home of Harry S. Truman. In 1950 he was the President of the United States of America, at the time of the Korean War, and I was a scholarship student sponsored by his administration. I went through his unpretentious home and closely looked at writings, photographs and memorabilia. I felt strongly that there was the essence of a most uncommon common man, no attempt to be other than what he was. These days, presidents are taken in by their own public relations experts.

Still on Interstate 70 we kept going straight west through Kansas into the foothills of Colorado. For about 2,400 miles we looked at never-ending wheat fields. They stretched to the horizon, blending into the sky in a golden haze. About every 400 miles we stopped for the day at a nice campsite. Invariably and first off I would clean the camper thoroughly while Janet prepared supper. I did most of the driving and reveled in it. The absolutely flat land has a beauty of its own. As the miles passed I imagined walking on the land, getting a feel for the enormity of this country. How could Germany try to stay equal to so much? Past and present thoughts and images moved through my mind. There I was almost 50 years after coming to the United States. To a certain extent and in a way I could now think of being an American. I am very aware of this dichotomy, two souls within myself. I always try to find the best that is within either.

Interstate 70 West begins to rise to the Colorado Rocky Mountain Ridge and reaches Pikes Peak at 14, 110 feet. I had been there in 1950 by car but now decided to take a cog railway up instead. Driving down from Pikes Peak I had listened to the car radio playing Beethoven's Funeral March that brought back sad memories. This time no emotions were involved but there was some concern regarding health. In 1950 I had noticed little difficulty with breathing but now I was decidedly uncomfortable just walking a few steps on the summit.

Down from the summit of Pikes Peak and along the front range there opens up an extraordinary national and natural landmark called The Garden of the Gods. Nature itself created very unusual red sandstone cliffs. Millions of years ago the landscape changed from being a mountain, to a sea and back to a mountain. Huge sandstone rocks were sculptured by the forces of erosion or perhaps the gods themselves did it. Janet and I walked through this extraordinary garden with its ancient odd-shaped junipers and the white stocks of blooming yucca. We saw just one tourist walking by. She happened to have one of those classic Hellenic faces. It struck us that there might be an incarnation of a goddess wandering about in her garden but she went on and the image faded yet the memory remains.

Years ago when Walter was 15, we decided to ski during the winter break in Alta and Snowbird resorts near Salt Lake City, Utah. There we had a very good time, especially with one day of helicopter skiing, the first time ever for both of us. Needless to say Walter did unbelievably well and I did not.

From the very top of Alta we hiked up a very steep and narrow ridge in brilliant sunshine. I stopped and remarked to Walter that I was 45 and a heart attack could be thought of, but we kept on going up. With memories like these Janet and I simply had to see Alta once more. The road going up the steep canyon with our camper showed increasingly smaller trees until finally we were at the highest campsite at 10,000 feet. Down in Salt Lake City it was above 100 degrees Fahrenheit; here it was cold at night and snow still remained under the picnic table. We hiked for days in meadows and rock outcroppings, relaxed in the evenings and looked at the stars in the firmament. Finally, we headed for home.

Seven years had gone by since my stroke. Many seasons had passed on Vancouver Island with long summers, beautiful autumns and springs, and short winters. Janet did her music and kept our home; I skied mostly at Whistler and kept doing some projects down at our waterfront. The two of us had fun thinking of new ventures abroad. We had travelled mostly with our beloved Westfalia which showed no signs of needing major repairs. Neither was there any indication of physical ills. My speech impediment remained more or less constant. I still could not adequately express what I felt like saying. For 1996 we decided to go on a boat tour and enjoy a new experience.

My sister Madi had been to our home on Vancouver Island and had travelled with us in Southern British Columbia. Now she invited us for a cruise down the Danube River from Passau to Budapest and back again. On the first and most scenic part of the river it turns and comes close to a very high and steep mountain. There a formidable old castle dominates the town of Durstein. In 1192 the local Baron waylaid and ransomed the English King Richard the Lionhearted as he came back from the Crusades. For hours we hiked all over the ruins and marveled at what still is a medieval site.

There were many other picturesque villages and landings. Spending time with my sister, Madi was much appreciated. In Budapest and Vienna the Danube landings allow one to come close to the inner cities, their buildings, monuments, parks and palaces. I felt we saw the essence of Budapest and Vienna each in its own way, in spite of only days in these beautiful cities. We left Vienna on a humorous note. After several hours of sight-seeing, Janet had to prevail on the tour guide to find a toilet. This lady said and I quote, "Either you see the palace or go to the toilet". There was no choice! I hung back as the tour group entered Schoenbrunn Palace and waited for Janet who soon found me. We were then able to enjoy the palace and its beautiful gardens.

Having been on the Danube cruise and liking the closeness of water and landscape, we decided in 1997 to try a real cruise. There would be two weeks in the Eastern Mediterranean and four weeks travelling in Europe. We also decided to drive the camper to Toronto and fly from there. This three-month undertaking would give us incredible memories and much to think about.

We flew to Munich, took the Eurail to Italy and the ferry from Brindisi to Greece. The good ship, Stella Solaris, a medium-sized cruise ship, took us first to Crete but not as before on a ferry sleeping on the open deck as ten years earlier. The Aegean islands of Rhodes and Patmos were explored and days spent on the island of Santorini, without doubt the incomparable crown jewel of them all. Fascinating places of antiquity in Asia Minor came to life, in particular at Ephessos. As usual, and as before we explored on our own but we also had meals and some excursions with agreeable fellow passengers.

During the second week, we sailed south to Alexandria and Cairo in perfect but very hot weather. On the boat, air conditioning at night helped but for the first time I experienced claustrophobia. I had to get up at night, go up on deck and stay there. The ship's doctor prescribed heavy-duty sleeping pills to assuage occasional anxiety feelings. It occurred to me that walking all over the place in this heat may not have been a good thing. At Ghiza, Janet suggested getting on a camel to see the pyramids. She sat very well riding hers. However, her camel bit mine, almost throwing me off. Then her camel's owner hit her camel with his whip and Janet was hanging on for dear life. When the camels settled down, we enjoyed the rest of our ride.

The time remaining at the pyramids and in Cairo itself is not clearly remembered by me. I recall constant bright sunshine and continuous high heat. I didn't pay that much attention to the palace or to all the statues in the Egyptian museum. As we left for the coast our bus passed an ugly cemetery. I felt quite relieved to get away from Cairo and back to our ship. I was not up to joining another bus tour the next day to Ashdod, Jerusalem and Bethlehem. As we continued north toward the Dardanelles, Troy and the Sea of Marmara the heat lessened and I felt much better by the time we arrived in Istanbul.

This is a beautiful metropolis unlike any other city, divided in two parts by the Bosporus, one part in Asia Minor and one part in Europe. Large European cities show growth in line with national and cultural identities. In Istanbul however you see not only two distinct parts but within each there are contradictory designs and buildings. Christian, Islamic and other influences abound. We walked through and admired the architecture of the Valens Aquaduct, the Suleymanique Mosque and the Blue Mosque, the Agia Sophia and the Topkapi Palace, to mention just the most important splendors. But there was one more to come. A carpet demonstration took place for passengers who wanted to examine and purchase items. The cruise company would guarantee reasonable value, quality and home delivery. I watched a dealer open a large heavy carpet, lift one border high up and bring it down, creating a ripple effect that flattened out. The motion caused the sky-blue beautiful silk material to glitter and reflect all its colours and its glory. This splendor could not possibly be stepped on, even if US$ 80,000 was no object! We had to leave; the Stella Solaris was on its way to Athens. On deck the Golden Horn of Istanbul was behind us as well as the magnificent buildings of the Christian and Ottoman past. A splendid cruise came to an end.

My favourite Eurail transportation took us from Brindisi to Florence. It was the city Janet liked most and we could stay there for weeks any time. My cultural acumen was not really developed when I was younger. Later on I was more fortunate and able to learn and appreciate the better things in life. In Avignon, there was an interval of rest and enjoyment, looking at fabulous tapestries in the papal residence and eating in outdoor cafes. Then we took the train to Barcelona, Spain. Our hotel was just off the main street. We entertained ourselves royally. There were guided city tours and attractions, excellent food, authentic Flamenco dancing and a variety of street acts every night.

Travelling back to France and into Nice, I wanted to take a secondary train through a very scenic but twisting route going up into the maritime alps and into Torino, Italy. Ever since fast European trains became streamlined and windows sealed I preferred slower trains allowing me to lean out a bit and sniff the air. The lure of riding the train started many years ago when I did not have money for a ticket. These days I still love taking the train. Janet also likes the ease of moving from one country to another but perhaps less determinedly.

Leaving our Torino hotel with our luggage for the train to Milano we got separated and lost each other. A huge demonstration was taking place, bands were playing, people pushing, yelling and letting off fireworks as I desperately tried to recognize streets. I got increasingly disoriented and very upset. Ever since being in artillery positions that kept on firing I just cannot take very loud noises. I managed to find a taxi but I could not name the hotel or find it. At the train station several hours later I could not explain anything so I simply sat down and waited for Janet who came and found me.

Later on it occurred to me that this might have been some sort of wake-up call but I did not feel any such thing at the time. After a short day in Milano and several days hiking around the Italian-Swiss border at Bellinzona we went back to experience the beautiful upper Italian lakes such as Lago Maggiore. A bus took us east to Tirano and north via the Bernina Express to St. Moritz, Davos and Chur, a most spectacular one-day railroad experience. It kept me looking left and right out the window all day long. At night the close-by church bell at Chur woke us up every quarter hour. Chur was less than a day away from Arosa and another cog railway opportunity. Ten years ago by camper we had a beautiful time in the Swiss mountains but now had to keep to our northern European plan.

Janet had not yet been to Marburg where I lived with my uncle as a youngster. I had been there several times. Now we took this opportunity for her to see and experience what I had mentioned and described to her so many times. The two of us together walked through the old cobblestone streets, up to the steep fortified castle where Martin Luther's desk and inkwell stood, down to the nearby Lutheran Church and its beautiful old manse. Through the mist of memory I see my Uncle Schmidmann and his wife as I lived so happily with them between the ages of nine and eleven. Janet shared my longing for what was so much of my past. It was nostalgia time in Marburg.

The next part of the European trip started with a first-ever overnight train ride to Berlin in a two-bed compartment but I did not sleep well. Fifty-five years ago in the army in 1942 I remember a beautiful spring. Now it was cold, rainy and unpleasant. Perhaps I could only think about the unbelievable fighting and destruction that took place, or the attempt to completely dismantle all of Germany and its remaining heritage. Germany now literally rose from the past but I would have preferred to observe the transformation some other time. We took an extended bus tour then decided on another night train to Malmo in Sweden and the express to Stockholm where Janet recuperated for two days. As in Switzerland I walked about in Stockholm thinking that there was no indication of a war having taken place for centuries. Some people may say that this was due to more consistent peaceful pursuits. It should be pointed out that a given nation may be situated on the periphery of large geographic units or isolated within it. More populous tribes occupied the centre of Europe establishing individual hegemonies and later large nation states. To blame the Germans for doing most of the fighting is in vogue these days, politically correct but historically incorrect.

A huge ferry to Helsinki took about twenty hours and was partly paid for by the Eurail system. Apparently a lot of Swedes make use of this popular excursion for entertainment and excellent food all weekend long. I have seldom allowed myself to overeat but this time I did. Perhaps subconsciously I prepared for Russian food in St. Petersburg! In Helsinki and upon returning there, we were most impressed by this clean, bright northern city, its well-maintained public buildings and residences, its parks and monuments such as that of Sibelius. I feel one could stay, live there and become part of Helsinki. Quite different observations were noted as we travelled to St. Petersburg. The train had a somewhat used diesel engine and its coaches needed cleaning. On sidings equipment appeared not to be in good repair or improperly stacked. Rails were not welded so the train swayed and was noisy. This was a main line first-class train but did not come close to those used in Europe. As we pulled into St. Petersburg I saw myself going back in time fifty-six years to the place near Moscow in the war when I was seventeen. I was allowed to stay in a first-aid station overnight, then was transferred all the way back to Germany. My unit was wiped out, all my comrades gone and with them many of my connections to the past.

Except for our cruise and having to pre-book our hotel in St. Petersburg, most of our travelling plans were relatively unstructured giving us the freedom to be adventurous as opportunity arose. Now was the time to see something of Russia and its people. The ones we met were invariably friendly and kind to us. Not just young people but middle-aged ones as well would get up to let Janet have a seat but usually I kept standing to keep fit. At times there was a little smile on a fellow fitness buff's face. More than once some person would come up from behind to help us settle directions. The use of the Cyrillic alphabet for street names and buses, and maps not to scale added to our difficulties. Down in the subway we wanted to go in one direction but were told to go in another. I kept insisting but the Russians did as well. After a lot of pointing to the map in my hand, a bystander speaking some English explained that the subway junction had flooded and we had to take a different route. I looked at the Russian and indicated it was one for Russia, nothing for Canada.

Having had difficulties being in a large group of sightseers with just one guide as at Schoenbrunn Palace, we were determined to find a personal guide at the Hermitage. We looked around the main entrance and staircase observing what appeared to be students working there. We found Natalya, who did art restorations and hired her for several days. She turned out to be very knowledgeable and a delight to be with. For the first time I could look at and understand some art that was explained to me in simple terms and slowly. The Hermitage did not turn me into a connoisseur but did give me a touch of understanding in art.

The best from all over the world was there at the Hermitage—paintings, sculpture, antiques, furniture, clocks, gold and silver displays, all in the five buildings that made up the winter palace. There were incredible interior decorations in a profusion of reception rooms, halls and staircases. There were masses of white marble and ancient Roman mosaic floors. I could not help but think of all the artisans who caused this incredible wealth to come about. Countless serfs drained the swamps, built the city and created St. Petersburg for the glory of Peter the Great and Russia. Now we can look at and admire all this beauty but should give some thought to the millions who toiled incessantly.

On a rare sunny day we took a local train to Peterhof, the Czar's summer palace about 20 kilometres outside St. Petersburg. Many Russian families were on the train, carrying picnic baskets and all dressed up for their outing. We found out that entry to the beautiful, extensive grounds was free. The palace, heavily bombed during the war, has been meticulously restored. We had an excellent English tour guide.

On the other side of the palace, the ground slopes down to the lower park with a cascade of fountains that end at the Gulf of Finland where the Czar's barge occasionally landed to inspect progress. Inside and out, this extraordinary palace of the north impresses and overwhelms the one in Versailles. We finally left Peterhof tired but happy as we managed to get home to the hotel, thanks to a number of very helpful Russians. Every so often these days we take out our art pictures and delight in what we were allowed to see.

Additional visits to the Hermitage, the Russian Museum and an outing to see the famous circus with Irina (an hotel employee who befriended us) rounded out our stay in St. Petersburg. From our eleven-storey hotel Janet took a last photo of the nearby St. Isaac's Cathedral at eleven o'clock at night. The city and the northern sky were still light, the sunlight reflecting and glittering on St. Isaac's dome in the "white night" of St. Petersburg. We will remember this extraordinary city and hope to return. A train took us to Helsinki, a plane to Amsterdam and then to Toronto where we picked up our camper and drove it home to Maple Bay, 4,550 km.

15

THE LAST CHAPTER

Walter's first-born son Justen was born in 1997. Shortly thereafter I was given an angiogram and a quintuple by-pass. Evidently I always had a strong heart but arteries had been constricted due to bad eating habits and heavy smoking for decades. I made a quick recovery and soon went heli-skiing again. For some time I allowed myself to imagine I could now live for decades.

For almost ten years, I had been at ease without mental stress, on permanent holidays as it were. With good friends and Janet's love and support, I was living well. While this could continue I had a feeling that a somewhat more purposeful life should be contemplated.

One day Walter quite casually remarked that I should remember and write down what I had experienced over the many years. Several ideas started to come up but I hesitated. I could see and draw images in my mind, but to come up with words and put them in writing was very difficult.

After all, in 1988 after a stroke, I had had a very real struggle just to talk again. Could I now come up with, at least some of the time, the right words and sentences? Could they stay in memory and not be irretrievably lost in the mind? Would I still be able to apply correct grammar and logic? Should I make any attempt to write given my sudden mental breakdowns and interrupted thinking? I felt a challenge would be worthwhile and my grandson would remember me better. I decided to write.

First it looked like I would do well, especially with the opening chapters of dramatic content. Then it became apparent that the right words were there but sentences had to be found and composed with increasing effort. I tried to write well but had to cope with constant stroke-related interruptions. It did not help that everything had to be hand-written and corrected several times. Using a computer was impossible for me. When finally a sentence or paragraph was found to my liking I was pleased with myself. At other times, close to tears of frustration, even I had to question all this mental commotion. I did my best and occasionally delighted in my work. When you write about your life you actually live it once more.

It is difficult to write about those who died. Would that they could hear what I now say about them. I think of the affection and concern that I did not bestow on my sister, Madi. She died in 1998 in Seeshaupt. I should have been a more concerned brother and more loving. I stayed away when I could have visited more often. My brother-in-law was not capable of providing the spirit and happiness which she so desperately needed. Our mother was always impartial with us but the gods were not and preferred me. They allowed her only a minimum of happiness in her life. After her husband died she remarried in the spring of 1997 but only had one happy year. I will always remember the good times we had together.

Mark Kingsbury and his wife Marion worked for CMH, he as its president. On May 25, 2001, Mark was killed instantly in an accident. I came to this site only hours later and looked at his bloodstains on the pavement. Strong feelings came up for Mark but as well for my best friend who was killed sixty years ago during the war on Monte Casino, Italy. I did not really know Mark but through Walter and the company a close association developed. I came to identify with him. The inscrutable gods of heaven called on Mark to leave in the prime of his years. I still think of my friend of long ago but also now of Mark and Marion.

The millennium had now arrived. I found out I was still alive much to my surprise although, like other people, I had proceeded at times under the assumption that I would always be around. A bit of wisdom has come to me late in life and not without trials and tribulation.

My story begins in Arosa, Switzerland and comes to a close on Vancouver Island, Canada. German was spoken first, then English. After a debilitating stroke neither language could be spoken coherently. Then English was slowly and painfully acquired once more and German renewed. Through writing, my mind and spirit improved. I was allowed to think again. May readers appreciate this story; may my loved ones be as happy as I always was.

Justen and Teagan Bruns

To My Grandchildren

Against All Might And All Odds
Never Falter, Ever Be Stronger
And The Gods Will Come To Your Aid

Goethe

Allen Gewalten Zum Trotz Sich Erhalten
Nimmer Sich Beugen, Kraftig Sich Zeigen
Rufet Die Arme Der Gotter Herbei

ISBN 1412033046-7

CPSIA information can be obtained
at www.ICGtesting.com
Printed in the USA
FSHW011604221120
76058FS

9 781936 639762